AMERICANA LIBRARY

ROBERT E. BURKE, EDITOR

AMERICANA LIBRARY

THE DEFLATION
of
AMERICAN IDEALS
An Ethical Guide for New Dealers

BY

EDGAR KEMLER

Introduction by Otis L. Graham, Jr.

UNIVERSITY OF WASHINGTON PRESS

SEATTLE AND LONDON

Acknowledgements

I wish to express my indebtedness to Mr. H. L. Mencken, Mr. I. F. Stone of *The Nation*, Prof. Max Lerner of Williams College, Prof. C. J. Friedrich and Dr. E. Pendleton Herring of Harvard University, and Dr. Rupert Emerson, Director of the Division of Territories in the Department of the Interior, for reading parts or all of the manuscript and suggesting improvements.

I also wish to thank Senator George L. Radcliffe of Maryland and his staff for allowing me to watch the processes of the federal government at close quarters during my period of composition; and Miss E. Keith Glenn and Mr. Joseph Swire for editorial assistance.

EDGAR KEMLER

Cambridge, Mass.

Contents

Introduction

At the beginning of Franklin Roosevelt's New Deal one could be sure there was to be reform—but of what variety, according to what plan, no one seemed to know. The forecast had changed with the Democratic candidate's mood and audience, but upon his election the word went out that Walter Lippmann's "unqualified" but "amiable man" from Albany was a man of progressive temperament, and that the climate in Washington was to be congenial to the projects of those who identified themselves as reformers. As the President indeed proved open-minded and experimental, glad of any idea so long as it promised action, so the New Deal was eclectic from the start, embracing a variety of reform creeds and approaches which to tidier minds often seemed actually contradictory.

To formulate and administer his many-sided assault on a discredited status quo, Roosevelt enlisted reformers of all types. Old Wilsonians like Josephus Daniels, Bull Moosers like Harold Ickes, Insurgents like George Norris, city planners like Frederic Delano, young planners in the C. H. Van Hise–Herbert Croly tradition like Rex Tugwell and Adolph Berle, veterans of the coordinating agencies of the war effort like Hugh Johnson, social workers like Frances Perkins and Harry Hopkins, northeastern urban politicians like Robert Wagner—all jostled one another in the councils of the New Deal. With the new bureaucrats and informal advisers so diverse in background and ideology, with the New Deal

equally diverse in its legislative experiments, it was easy to
wonder just what *was* a New Dealer. They rarely seemed to
agree, they came from different backgrounds and pulled in
different directions, and often did not like each other. New
Dealer Tugwell spoke for governmental coordination of an
economy of large business units, but New Dealer Thurman
Arnold sought prosperity by a zealous enforcement of the
antitrust acts. New Dealer Henry Morgenthau yearned to
restore investor confidence with a balanced budget, but New
Dealer Marriner Eccles pushed for a deliberate federal defi-
cit. An alert newsman could list the New Dealers, as John
Franklin Carter ("The Unofficial Observer") did in *The
New Dealers,* or Joseph Alsop and Robert Kintner did in
Men Around the President, but no one had much success in
generalizing about them.[1] If there was such a thing as a New
Dealer, as a new liberalism, it resisted ideological definition.
Observers in the 1930's knew that New Deal liberalism was
not merely the old progressivism, although plainly it bor-
rowed the earlier rhetoric and experience. They knew that
the intellectual arsenal of reform in the 1930's contained
many elements, some of them new, most of them contradictory. They found it difficult to describe the whole in the
language of even a reasonably coherent political ideology.

Eight years after Roosevelt took office, a young Harvard-
educated liberal named Edgar Kemler, in a book called *The
Deflation of American Ideals,* seemed to have found the
common denominator. By ignoring intramural disputes over
programs and measures and focusing upon qualities of mind
and temperament, Kemler differentiated the new reformer
from the old. Where the older progressivism (Kemler used
the terms "progressivism" and "liberalism" carelessly, but

[1]John Franklin Carter, *The New Dealers* (New York: Simon and Schuster,
1934), and Joseph Alsop and Robert Kintner, *Men Around the President* (New
York: Doubleday, Doran, 1939).

it was clear that by progressivism he meant the Theodore
Roosevelt–Wilson era and by liberalism the New Deal variety) sought primarily ethical and moral goals, the new liberalism concentrated almost exclusively upon the repair of the
economic system. Where the older progressivism had been
self-righteous in tone and perfectionist and utopian in ex-
pectation, New Deal liberalism was piecemeal, sophisticated,
hardened against failure and disappointment by a realistic
outlook. Where progressivism sought individual improvement, the New Deal thought in terms of social forces and
institutions.

The change had taken place, Kemler thought, at the end
of the Progressive era. Earlier reformers — Mugwumps,
Populists, most progressives—had been mired in crusades
for moral uplift. But toward the end of progressivism, Kemler argued, a few progressives began to grow less interested
in righteousness and more interested in an efficient economy.
One could see this change taking place under both Theodore
Roosevelt and Wilson, for both men seemed to shift toward
economic and away from moral concerns near the end of
their tenures in office. A further evidence of this new orien-
tation was their accommodation with the professional politicians, as they realized that results could only be gained
through the hardheaded employment of a disciplined party,
however impure a professional political party might be. Re-
flecting this trend in the thought and practice of the two
Presidents, dispassionate intellectuals and engineers began
to outnumber the clergymen and apostles of moral uplift.

But this promising start of the emancipation from moral-
ism made no substantial progress during the 1920's, so far as
Kemler could see, and it required a depression to complete
the reorientation of progressivism. After 1929 there was no
time for pious denunciations of this or that immoral practice.
Now reformers fought single-mindedly to revive the econ-

omy. They were on no trek to a Heavenly City where men looked to their civic duties because they had heard the call of conscience. United by the new focus on gross national product figures and production curves, and enjoying a new flexibility because of their disdain for moral judgments, the New Dealers—pragmatic, confident without being utopian, technicians rather than sermonizers—were much more formidable than the progressives had ever been.

This same temper, so necessary in keeping the attention of reformers fixed upon the main problem in domestic affairs —the material wants of needy people—gave the liberals an advantage also in foreign policy. No believers in the fine idealistic reasons for American entry into World War I, they were not subject to the disillusionment that made isolationists of so many, but could see that prosaic matters of national security dictated a policy of collective security. By 1941, when Kemler published his book, liberals were ready to marshal America's technical and industrial resources for the life struggle with fascism.

Kemler claimed to be writing history—"the history of progressive idealism in America"—but *The Deflation of American Ideals* should be seen primarily as an original source for the historian of the New Deal and the larger liberal reform tradition. Kemler himself was by no means a typical New Dealer. A resident of H. L. Mencken's Baltimore and a 1936 graduate of Johns Hopkins, he had worked for a time with *The Nation,* where he knew Max Lerner and I. F. Stone. He left *The Nation* for the Littauer School at Harvard, and earned a Master's Degree in Public Administration in 1941. His government experience consisted of a brief stint with Senator George Radcliffe (Maryland Democrat), far removed from the excitement and decision making at the other end of Pennsylvania Avenue. But if not an important liberal, Kemler was at least a dedicated one, and he possessed the combination of New Deal enthusiasms and historical perspective necessary to produce one of the first descriptions of the temper that distinguished New Deal liberalism.

Kemler spoke of and for a new mentality, depuritanized by its urban origins, deutopianized by the disappointments of the war and the shocks administered by the evidence of human meanness that postwar Europe continually presented. He spoke for young men and women too busy fighting privation and even starvation to expend energies on moral uplift, under no illusions that the battle for a better life could be won by a courteous appeal to individual consciences. The liberalism he expressed assumed the invalidity of the old truths, and therefore found it easy, in the emergency of the 1930's, to disregard ancient prohibitions against unbalancing the budget, tampering with the Court, drawing professors and atheists into public service, and putting government into the business of selling electricity or building towns. The humanitarian ideals of their reform predecessors were still present, but what made the new reformism post-progressive was the impact made upon its methods and its operating assumptions by two intellectual currents which the progressives had largely escaped, realism and relativism.

I use the term "realism" here to denote not so much the emphasis upon the material, which affected progressives more than Kemler knew,[2] but a more pessimistic view of human nature and the prospects for individual and social improvement. This gloomier view of man, owing less to Freud than to the War and its aftermath, led some progressive intellectuals to despair of politics altogether (e.g., Herbert Croly), but more often it led to a different political alignment. As the evidence for man's depravity accumulated, some left

[2]See Robert Bremner, *From the Depths: The Discovery of Poverty in the United States* (New York: New York University Press, 1956).

the gradualist politics and capitalistic economics of the progressives for faiths that promised to change the fundamentals (e.g., Lincoln Steffens), and others veered to the right in fright at the potentialities of state power in the hands of puny, untrustworthy human beings (e.g., Walter Lippmann).

But most younger intellectuals, like Kemler, assimilated the new view of man without losing their confidence in the melioristic use of the state within a capitalistic order. A large part of the importance of *The Deflation* lies in its forceful expression of the view that the flawed nature of man required neither a total overturn of society nor a rejection of any public action, but a welfare state alternative.[3] Speaking for the jaunty followers of Roosevelt, Kemler reasoned from a pessimistic anthropology to an appreciation of the need for coercion when persuasion failed, the inevitability of selfish power, and the possibility of fashioning a more viable social order through the manipulation of power groups and interests. Thus the distinguishing qualities of New Deal liberalism: pessimistic enough to be elitist, skeptical, quick to turn from persuasion to compulsion; never pessimistic enough to be fatalistic. It resembled the controlled pessimism of that very hopeful generation of realists, the Founders, and Kemler's book is one of the signs that liberalism had returned, full circle, to the tenth *Federalist*.

The Deflation is an especially useful specimen of the New Deal mind for yet another reason. The progressives made way for their own reforms by attacking the status quo in law and philosophy with a corrosive relativism, but we know from reading Eric Goldman, David Noble, Charles Forcey, and

---

[3]A more important thinker, Reinhold Niebuhr, arrived at this position by the end of the Second World War: see his *Children of Light and Children of Darkness* (New York: Scribner, 1944). In his seminal book, *Moral Man and Immoral Society* (New York: Scribner, 1932), Niebuhr argued that a realistic view of man committed the Christian thinker to democratic socialism, a position he held throughout the New Deal.

Morton White[4] that the progressive mind sometimes drifted into confusion when it entered a constructive phase. The postwar intellectual problems of progressives like Carl Becker, Vernon L. Parrington, and Harold Stearns testify to the shortcomings of a relativistic pragmatism to provide firm goals for reformers once the enemy was in retreat. However true this may have been for the more thoughtful progressives, *The Deflation* demonstrates how a younger, perhaps less scrupulously logical thinker could escape the disorientation of his elders. Kemler's liberal was exhilarated by the knowledge that nothing was permanently true or good, and took it as an invitation to maneuver in formerly forbidden areas. He assumed that his goal was recovery (notice that he was completely uninterested in any discussion of how one arrived at this goal, or any other), and turned with relish to the congenial task of planning his next move. Liberalism may have seemed philosophically rudderless to some prominent twentieth-century thinkers, but Kemler reminds us in *The Deflation* that this did not bother the average New Dealer. Kemler himself was deeply involved in the Negro movement up until his death in 1960, evidence that the humanistic ideals inherited by New Deal liberalism were too well rooted to be damaged by the relativistic component of liberal thought.

As history, *The Deflation* is in many ways an unsatisfactory performance. It is flawed by minor errors, such as the date of Beard's *An Economic Interpretation of the Constitution of the United States* (1913, not 1908), or the date when Teddy Roosevelt moved against the Northern Securities Corporation (1902) and Standard Oil (1906). Whatever put an end to muckraking, it was not Beard's book, as

[4]Eric Goldman, *Rendezvous with Destiny* (New York: Knopf, 1952); David Noble, *The Paradox of Progressive Thought* (Minneapolis: University of Minnesota Press, 1958); Charles Forcey, *Crossroads of Liberalism* (New York: Oxford University Press, 1961); Morton White, *Social Thought in America* (New York: Oxford University Press, 1949).

Kemler claimed (p. 63). More seriously, *The Deflation* is
written with an aggressive disdain for qualifications. The new
interests and temper of mind which characterized liberalism
came neither so suddenly nor so pervasively into the reform
mind as Kemler suggests. One would never guess from the
book that there were New Dealers who were morally opposed to alcohol (e.g., Josephus Daniels), unpragmatically
devoted to the Constitution (e.g., Raymond Moley) or to
honesty and good administration (e.g., Harold Ickes), even
so inflexible and unpragmatic as to become Communists (e.g.,
Alger Hiss). Indeed, he never admits that the New Dealers
were insufficiently pragmatic and technically proficient to
succeed at their primary task, recovery. And while ignoring
those New Dealers who were not so deflated after all, he
fails to mention that there were many progressives—for example, Florence Kelley, Paul Kellogg, John Haynes Holmes,
Ben Lindsey—who had from the very beginning of their reform careers worked only for the hard-headed goals of improved living and working conditions, and not at all for
moral uplift.

Another serious error is Kemler's lack of interest in the
1920's, which he saw as a time of little change in the progressive mind. As an admirer of Mencken he should have known
how important were the years of the 1920's in deflating the
idealisms he was so glad to be rid of in the 1930's. He ignored the political alteration of the Democratic party that
went forward quietly in the years after the war (Al Smith's
career might have served as a portent), just as he ignored
the substantial intellectual advances made by the social welfare wing of the Progressive movement, described for us so
well by Clarke Chambers.[5]

But whatever his errors, Kemler had described with ad-

[5]Clarke Chambers, *Seedtime of Reform: American Social Service and Social
Action, 1918-1933* (Minneapolis: University of Minnesota Press, 1963).

mirable clarity and timeliness an important turning point in
the history of reform in America—the transition from progressivism to liberalism. He saw that the New Dealer was in
important ways a new type, and he described the characteristics of the New Deal collective mind in a fashion that his-
torians have subsequently ratified. Because of this perspective, Kemler saw the apparently inexplicable opposition of
old progressives to the New Deal for what is was—consistency. He was not surprised when surviving progressives,
like William E. Borah and Oswald Garrison Villard, "cluttered up the progressive army with their vestigial reputations," unable to make the shift from moral indignation to
"filling the animal needs of the community."

Kemler was not the first liberal intellectual to be critical
of the progressives—the autobiographies of Frederic C.
Howe and Lincoln Steffens had undertaken that, along with
John Chamberlain's *Farewell to Reform,* published in 1932.
But his book is the first I know of to argue that Norris was
the exception and Borah the rule, an insight into the attitude
of the balance of surviving progressives toward the New
Deal which I have found, in my *An Encore for Reform,* to
be substantially correct.[6] While Kemler undoubtedly exaggerated the degree of difference, it was just such a tempera-
mental gap which Richard Hofstadter took into account,
along with other evidence, in constructing his persuasive
argument for progressivism–New Deal discontinuity in *The
Age of Reform.*[7]

Perhaps Kemler caught his insight during his days with
The Nation, where he could have seen the prototypes of the
old and new reformers side by side: the aging Oswald Gar-

[6]Otis L. Graham, Jr., *An Encore for Reform: The Old Progressives and the
New Deal* (New York: Oxford University Press, 1967).

[7]Richard Hofstadter, *The Age of Reform* (New York: Alfred A. Knopf,
1955).

rison Villard, old-fashioned in dress and manner, operating within the limits of Mugwumpery to the last, distrustful of F.D.R., the New Deal, modern literature, and the new militant mood taking over the NAACP;[8] and, on the same staff but eager to take the magazine far from Villard's social and political views, younger liberals like Freda Kirchwey and Max Lerner and I. F. Stone, chafing against Villard's political vacillations and his negativism and his prudery, shocking the old man in the 1930's by aligning the magazine with the domestic New Deal, collective security, and the franker forms of modern poetry and fiction.

Certainly Kemler exaggerated the characterological consistency of both progressivism and liberalism, was oddly complacent about the philosophical shallowness of a reformism too busy and too proud to give thought to its ends, and seemed uninterested in learning precisely where and how the new mental qualities had intervened in the reform experience. But *The Deflation* is nonetheless one of the landmarks —along with a few books of even greater stature such as Croly's *The Promise of American Life* or Veblen's *The Theory of the Leisure Class* or Niebuhr's *Moral Man and Immoral Society*—of the history of modern reform thought. Judging from the style, *The Deflation* was aimed at a larger audience than it received, and its timing partially accounts for its relatively obscurity. It did not change minds so much as it expressed a changed mind. As Richard Hofstadter said of another book quite like it in spirit, Thurman Arnold's *The Folklore of Capitalism*, it represents a "statement of the working mood of a great many New Dealers." *The Deflation of American Ideals* stands as a contemporary expression

---

[8]A fine account of Villard in his final years may be found in Michael Wreszin, *Oswald Garrison Villard: Pacifist at War* (Bloomington: Indiana University Press, 1965).

of the dominant faith of the American intellectual and political elite as the nation readied its physical and intellectual resources for the test of war.

OTIS L. GRAHAM, JR.

February, 1967
Santa Barbara, California

PART I

———

PROLOGUE

CHAPTER ONE

Political Animalism

1. AMERICA IN THE FASCIST ERA

THERE can be little doubt that Europe has fallen on evil days. You might even say that she is politically decadent. In Germany, Italy, Russia, Spain and the smaller States, fine old institutions have been either overthrown or twisted to new purposes—churches, trade unions, schools, newspapers, political parties, constitutions, and in some places, capitalism, itself. Nor has anything very wonderful emerged from this wreckage except the careers of a handful of adventurers.

We in America remain true to our heritage. We still cherish the institutions that were established with the founding of the Republic—our free worship, free schools, freedom of speech, our two-party system and Constitution, and even our capitalism, which, if somewhat chastened, still survives. Yet with the destruction of France and the beleaguering of England, the last great democracies of Europe, we carry on in the New World, set apart by two unsatisfactory oceans, in an atmosphere that makes our very virtue seem rare and fragile.

It is no wonder that we too have begun to slip. We have, I believe, acquired something of the decadent temper that goes with the destruction of those institutions abroad. Day in and day out we deplore the corruption of Germany and Russia. But the more we deplore, the more we are ourselves tainted. We are like the missionary in Somerset Maugham's *Rain*, who, deploring the immorality of the fallen woman, imperceptibly became ensnared in her very charm.

We can, of course, stop trading with totalitarians, throw out all their agents and sympathizers, and sunder diplomatic relations. We might even succeed in a quarantine of their system of government, but we cannot quarantine their values. Dictatorial volcanoes have been bursting through the constitutional surface of Europe, and the dust and debris has been drifting over and saturating the atmosphere we live in. We cannot retain our poise in the presence of primitive forces. We cannot make love like a Puritan in the midst of an orgy. Nor can we conduct democracy like Mugwumps as long as other governments are conducting their affairs with violence.

The wonder of it is not that we have been affected by Fascist morality, but that we have resisted as well as we have. One does not have to be a Spengler to see everywhere evidence of the decline of the West. Since the turn of the century, and especially since the First World War, the eternal verities that held up the spacious universe of the nineteenth century have been crumbling away. The old ultimates of matter and energy have turned out to be vague, imponderable wisps. And the solid framework of Newton has been distorted beyond recognition by the curved space and four dimensions of Einstein.

Just as our outer universe has changed, so have our standards and conduct in the inner universe. In the arts, the old academies have been overthrown by cubism, futurism, and surrealism. In morality, Victorian standards have given way before the attack of psychoanalysis and post-war disillusionment. In politics, we have not only discarded gold standards and balanced budgets, once the cardinal principles of good government; we have even begun to question constitutional government itself.

But through all this flux our eighteenth-century conception of democracy has remained relatively unchanged. Only now have we begun adjusting ourselves to the new moral atmosphere. Though we still pay homage to the same gods and the same fundamental law, something of the new spirit has crept into our political thinking and practices and deflated some of our premises almost without our consciousness. In a cynical age even the American democratic ideal, as expounded by its best representatives, has turned slightly cynical.

This is nothing to be alarmed about. The impact of the new moral climate has been, on the whole, beneficial. For we have deflated the unnecessary and obstructive things to the advantage of the essential. In the fire of ideological rivalry and depression, democracy stands clear of its trimmings and all the more powerful. Watching the development of Fascism and Communism, we can see the raw materials of human nature by which political adventurers rise, and we can judge by comparison the basic materials on which our own institutions have endured, and on which they must continue to endure in the stormy days ahead.

Many observers have commented on the impact of Fascism upon the New Deal. At the innovation of the NRA, there was considerable debate among them whether it was nascent Fascism or nascent Socialism. And even when the democratic purpose of the First New Deal became clear, these observers seemed to find considerable moral kinship with the totalitarian regimes in its disregard of precedent and of spiritual values. Far from welcoming the salutary effects, many screamed to high heaven—foremost among them, Dorothy Thompson. She wrote:

> "The idea that reform owes its vitality to the recognition of moral principles is rejected by most of our reformers, who see not the slightest connection between ends and means, between ideals and conduct. It is not considered indecent to use the most ruthless methods to assassinate the character of one's opponents. There is one conception of justice for the rich, another for the poor. Violence is justified in the hands of one group, denounced in the hands of another. The most high-handed actions of the economic royalists are adopted unquestioningly by the emerging class of political royalists."[1]

In the spring of 1940, with the overwhelming German victory over French and British arms, Fascism suddenly made a new and more resounding impact on American life. If there is doubt as to the character of the first impact, there can be no doubt at all as to that of the second. For with Fascism triumphant on the shores of the Atlantic Ocean, the rivalry has taken the form, not simply of ideal against ideal, but now of nation against nation. Fascism has become an imperial threat to our dominant position in the New World. Many of the same observers who deplored the impact of Fascism in a period of domestic reform have accepted the inevitability of the Fascist impact in a period of preparedness—foremost again, Dorothy Thompson, who thus became one of the most effective proponents of a third term for the deflater of American ideals, President Roosevelt.

By necessity the crisis has warped our efforts in the same direction in which Fascist efforts are warped. It has made us concentrate our energies on economic and military mobilization of men and resources. It has stirred a kind of nationalist hysteria which ferrets out the enemy at home and shouts defiance at the enemy abroad. And it has threatened such democratic values as our civil liberties and the advance of labor standards. Yet this menace has produced one beneficial effect. It has come so sharply and so abruptly that we have been forced to abandon the moral concerns that have traditionally befuddled our foreign policy. Now one can see the necessity for action in all its naked realism.

It is one of the bitter ironies that, as base metal drives out good, so a debased system of government drives out or debases a more noble system. I do not mean that by fighting a Fascist country we ourselves become Fascist. There is ample reason to believe that our system of government is resilient enough to survive great crises. But it is certainly true that in meeting the menace of the totalitarians we are momentarily accepting their values and challenging them on their own level. One scoundrelly nation run wild in the community of nations sets the rules for all the rest. Those who fail to accept those rules and to prove themselves more adept at the scoundrel's game will not survive. This much we have learned from the fate of the European democracies.

2. ANGELICISM VS. ANIMALISM

When the history of Western civilization will have been written, it will probably appear that we have lived in a Corrupt Age (1920–1940) comparable to nothing since the Renaissance. For the creeds now flourishing are the most naked and least exalted that man can believe in. They presuppose not that man is made in the likeness of God, replete with dignity, tolerance and rationality, but that he is simply the highest anthropoid, wallowing in racial egotisms, greed, power, and sensuality. These, I say, are the least exalted beliefs that a man can have. For if he

went any lower, he would regard himself as simple vegeta-
tion, unthinking and inanimate, and he would wilt for lack
of nourishment. For only vegetables are complete nihilists.

These animalic creeds prevail both in our private and our
public morality. Where sex has been the crux of conduct
in the one sphere, power has been the crux of conduct in the
other. And yet I believe that, though a life devoted to
sexual pleasure or a government devoted to self-aggrandize-
ment may be far from perfect, it at least is a starting point
for a satisfactory ethos. If man errs, he does not err so
much in yielding to his animal instincts as he does in trying
to assume a role of nobility for which his instincts are unsuited.

There seems to be some fateful discontent within us that
makes us impatient of our animal heritage. We are snobs
on an evolutionary scale—social climbing up the ladder of
species. Nor are we alone in our restlessness. The whole
animal kingdom seems to be a vast social whirl, where the
fish hope to be snakes, the snakes hope to be mice, the mice
hope to be monkeys, and the monkeys hope to be men. We
have arrived at the top, but we are not satisfied. So we
conjure out of our imaginations a species that is even
superior to ourselves, the angels, and we set them up in
heaven. And once we have conjured them, we insist on
breaking into their set. We mimic their manners, their
preoccupation with virtue, their altruism, sexlessness, and
benevolence. And those who are satisfied with the bio-
logical station into which they are born we dismiss as
devils, with tail, cloven feet and horns, and we make them
out to be lower than they are.

Evolutionary snobbery, I submit, has been the curse of
our race. We have spent centuries torturing ourselves and
denying our antecedents so as to attain angelic stature.
But, being unfitted for such heights, we are hypocrites. We

become animals in the kitchen through being angels in the parlor. And when we find the weight of such hypocrisy unbearable, we go through a moral revolution. We swing from extreme angelicism to extreme animalism and back again, with hardly a rest in between. By its very nature evolutionary snobbery does not allow moderation.

Since the First World War there has been a general collapse of values, of the Pollyanna spirit in politics and of the prudery in morals. The millions of men who fought and died in that war did not fight and die for democracy alone, or for a League of Nations or for the protection of little nations or for the profits of munition makers. Whether they knew it or not, they also fought to overthrow the dead weight of Victorian angelicism, which has been called by some people dignity, and by others hypocrisy. In this respect they did not die in vain. If anything, they succeeded too well. For both sexually and politically our values have been swinging to the other extreme in the past twenty-odd years.

3. THE DOWNWARD COURSE

What have been the steps in the downward course of our political life? "The Great War has thrown America back upon itself," Walter Weyl observed in 1917.

> "It has come as a test and a challenge to all our theories. Suddenly, yet subtly, it has shaken our optimism and undermined our faith in the peaceful progress of humanity."[2]

I should be oversimplifying the picture if I wrote that our post-war experiences came altogether unexpected. There had been prophets of doom and violence in that late afternoon of the Victorian and Edwardian Era—Henri Bergson, William James, George Sorel. Santayana once had occasion to point out that there was something unnatural about Teddy Roosevelt's enthusiasm for the "strenuous life."

If our civilization were well-rounded, the "strenuous life"
would be the normal way of life and would be accepted as
an everyday fact; we would no more make a fetish of it
than of eating and sleeping.

Yet, for all the wise words of Bergson and the others,
nothing was more alien to our political thinking than doom
and violence. In the election of 1912, for example, the
American people were offered a Republican Taft, a Progressive Roosevelt, a Democratic Wilson, and a Socialist
Debs. Despite differences of tempo, they were all going
in the same direction: they were all looking to the democratization of our political and economic institutions. None
of these candidates doubted that man was ultimately per-
fectible and that, as he became more perfect, society would
also become more perfect. The only stench in the climate
of values arose from occasional outbreaks of the syndicalists,
who were regarded and treated as outlaws, and from the
imperialist excesses which were far away.

But the First World War brought violence into our lives
and had to be somehow squared with the assumptions of
human benevolence. Those of the extreme left were the
first to draw conclusions; they gathered together in Switzer-
land and resolved to overthrow the capitalist system.
After smoldering in the idyllic pre-war atmosphere, revolutionary Marxism burst forth and became, with the success
of the Russian Revolution in 1917, a permanent factor in
the political climate. This was the first break from the
angelicism of the progressive cause. The Communists incorporated into their program a sense of the realities which
the progressives lacked. As regards tactics, they were
thoroughly animalic. Capitalists, they reasoned, were not
mere selfish moguls who could be overthrown by a wave
of indignation, as was assumed in the sunny pre-war days.

They were the manipulators of death-dealing instruments and could be successfully fought only on their own terms.

But although the Communists parted from the progressives in their techniques they remained progressives in their objectives, which they expounded with all the verve of a Grover Cleveland or a Woodrow Wilson. They asserted that once revolution had been achieved there would be a flowering of human brotherhood the like of which had never before been seen and the state as an instrument of force would wither away. After twenty-odd years of Communist control in Russia, they are still waiting for this consummation. Indeed, at the moment, they seem a long way off from a Progressive Era. Stalin has engaged in the shooting of his revolutionary colleagues and, since the outbreak of the Second World War, in power politics of the most inscrutable kind. Nevertheless the impact of Soviet Communism upon the world progressive movement has been highly exaggerated. It has not contradicted progressive principles so much as deferred their realization to a remote future.

When Fascism emerged in backward Italy in 1922 and in aggressive Germany in 1933, it was by no means an animalic preamble to a progressive program. It was the very negation of progressivism and defiantly confronted the idea of progress itself. On the surface, the Fascist ideal would seem to be a restatement of nationalism. When nations like Italy, Germany and Poland were atomized or absorbed into foreign empires, nationalism was good progressive doctrine. It was a noble thing that men like Mazzini and Wilson could contemplate every racial entity with its own government and the world, an assemblage of free peoples.

After the First World War the national ideal broke off sharply from the progressive ideal and threatened to destroy it. It was no longer a question of the right of national existence for all, but of the destiny of certain chosen nations, Italy and Germany, to conquer and master the world. The Germans laid claim to all territories ever occupied by Germans since the Middle Ages, which encompassed most of Europe from Paris to Moscow and the German settlements throughout the world. And where they were unable to find expression for their Germanism abroad, they found expression at home, rendering their blood pure before it became expansive, and so liquidated their non-Aryan minority. The Italians laid claim to all the glory that was Rome. Such claims went beyond law or reasonable necessity. They were based on the ghosts of historical memory.

Manifestly democratic institutions could not well survive under such obsessions. The world was conceived as divided among a lot of struggling tribes, all seeking *Lebensraum* with fire and sword. What good then are parliaments or constitutions or civil liberties? War is man's natural state and these things only impede its efficient progress. Thus the whole economy is put on a military basis and a dictatorship established. And just as war is permanent, so the dictatorship is permanent. Both means and ends become thoroughly animalic.

Why did the average Italian or the average German, who is not fundamentally different from the average American, accept all this? Because, we have been told, he was nationally humiliated, desperate for security, and without leadership in constitutional politics. Under such conditions men are prone to think less worthy thoughts than usual. After saying, "I am Napoleon," there is nothing easier than pointing to a leader and saying, "He is Napoleon and we are a Napoleonic people." You do not have to profess belief in abstractions like justice, humanity, altruism, or self-restraint. As an ideal, it requires the very minimum of vision or consideration. It is the ambition of an egomaniac restated for an entire nation.

Yet what great leaders have ever sought dominion over men with so little pretense of human ennoblement as have Mussolini and Hitler? Caesar came to Gaul spreading Roman law and Roman peace. Charlemagne became master of Western Europe as the champion of the Christian faith. Even Napoleon in his march to Moscow was proclaiming the noble doctrines of the French Revolution. Civilization —in name, at least—has often been on the side of conquerors. But Hitler marches with only the swastika of oppression and despotism on his banners. He is the destroyer *par excellence*. His power is based on the promise of greater wreckage after each triumph. Even the tyrants of the Italian Renaissance, despite their lack of principle, were at least patrons of great art. But Hitler in his public life is as devoid of any accoutrement above the animal level as Attila or the pirates of Barbary.

To be sure, Hitler sometimes screens his ambitions behind the language of our liberal civilization. He talks of "fighting the plutocratic nations", of "saving Europe from the Reds", of the "rights of oppressed German minorities". But he shifts these phrases like so many veils with such rapidity and with such skill that to all who look for any length of time, he is completely naked. Mussolini, who is even less modest in his demonic role, makes up in boldness what he lacks in effectiveness. For he is not only naked, but an exhibitionist to boot. When the Soviet-German Pact was signed it undermined the last pretense of Fascist righteousness. Yet the Italians acclaimed it with relish. "This was doubtless done on Italian advice" declared Virginio Gayda, Mussolini's spokesman. "It is pure Machiavellianism from the viewpoint of political philosophy."[3]

4. ANIMALISM IN POLITICAL THOUGHT

This is the downward course that we have experienced in the western world, and we have been almost completely unprepared for it.   Where could we turn for an explanation? The political thinkers of the past were almost all of angelic inclination; and in an age of animalism they shed little light.   They did not state their assumptions in so many words, but managed to include them at the strategic points of their philosophies.

Plato and Aristotle conceived that man in order to fulfill his potentialities must be rational.   And although not all men might attain to that estate, those that did were to be entrusted with high office and were to hold sway over those that did not.   Angelicism was founded in their very definition of mankind.

In the Roman and Christian traditions the great thinkers incorporated their estimate of mankind in what they called "natural law."   This was the law which governed human conduct, not by edict or by code, but by man's inherent sense of justice.   Just as this natural law was a copy of the divine law, so the wise civil law was a copy of natural law, argued such eminent men as St. Thomas, St. Augustine, and Bodin.   Richard Hooker put it very neatly when he said, "The Law of Reason is the law whereby man in all his actions is directed to the imitation of God."

In the seventeenth century natural law changed its content and appearance.   Thinkers like Locke and Rousseau talked of all men being endowed with certain natural rights, the rights of life, liberty, property and the pursuit of happiness.   They no longer started with God and deduced the necessary laws.   They started with natural man and his inalienable rights and God was incidental to the picture. Indeed, the natural man was a very vital concept at the founding of the American Republic, and we are only now making the discovery that democracy can survive without such a disguised and unnecessary angel.

Finally, the school of Marxian thought, which boasts that it is hard-headed and materialistic, still preserves a degree of incantation. Despite its bold analysis of the human materials of capitalist society, it still falters in its estimate of the human materials of proletarian society. For the proletarian man, once he is in control of things, apparently presents no new contradictions, or at least no predictable contradictions, and so must be considered on a plane with the angels.

On such assumptions "dream states" have been fashioned —Plato's aristocracy, St. Thomas' monarchy, Rousseau's democracy, and Marx's socialism. In so far as they have emerged from the dynamic forces of the day, they pointed the direction and led men towards new institutions and new systems of government. But somehow the reality has never quite fulfilled the dream, nor can it ever when the dream is of a remote land inhabited by improbable people. The sages of political thought have, for the most part, been less shrewd as observers than inspired as prophets.

Here and there, however, a political thinker has described what he has seen and devised programs which were not based on any untoward assumptions of human goodness. Such a man has dealt bluntly with the materials at hand, seeing the stupid and self-intoxicated tyrant where others wrote of idealized monarchs, and the brutish and ignorant mob where others assumed an idealized people. If we are to build a Good Society, these are the bricks, he has said, and there is no indication that they will turn to gold when the building is finished.

Upon the appearance of such a thinker the world is invariably shocked. What? Deny the principles of Greek rationality or Christian natural law? It would be worse than denying the sun's orbit around the earth, or the divine origin of the human race, or the sanctity of marriage, or the existence of God. Take away our belief in the lofty character of our laws and of our political destination, it was said, and the very prerequisites of organized society would crumble and civilization would be no more.

On these grounds the world has dismissed the Sophists, Machiavelli, Hobbes, and other explorers of political animalism. They were ejected from the gallery of philosophers, and shut away like skeletons in a closet. Hobbes, to be sure, though long regarded as an atheist and an untouchable, has been restored to light for his contributions to the doctrines of sovereignty and individualism. But Machiavelli, who explored political animalism, has been accorded neither the dignity of a niche nor even a definitive estimate. He survives today, a tantalizing voice from a strange world. These men, living in corrupt surroundings, saw through the angelicism of their predecessors only to have their discoveries ignored by the resurgent angelicism of their successors. But today the world of Machiavelli and Hobbes is not strange. It is the world we live in, and their experience provides almost the only light by which we might interpret our own experience.

It is not true, as some would have it, that civil society cannot be built or a workable program based on the assumptions of animalism. Nor is it true that all those who accept Machiavelli as their teacher are invariably reactionary. Machiavelli was, as he revealed himself in the *Discorsi*, a republican and a libertarian who had high regard for the government of the ancient Roman Republic. In the Italy of his day, however, he could devise no strategy by which he could directly achieve his ideals. So he did what every wise progressive does. He compromised. He appealed to a Florentine despot to unite all Italy; and he expounded all the necessary techniques in a book called *The Prince*. Yet, because he advocated what was, under the circumstances, the only practicable reform, he has been damned and scourged. A united Italy under a single despot on the order of a united Britain under Henry VIII might seem a small advance today. But certainly to Machiavelli it was very important. And Cavour, who finally saw the fulfilment of the dream and who was considered a great liberal, did not hesitate to pay his respects to the master.

5. UNHAPPY PROMISED LAND

The real prophets of the downward course were not, strictly speaking, political thinkers, but philosophers primarily concerned with the inadequacy of nineteenth century middle-class morality—de Gobineau, Nietzsche, Sorel, Spengler. Whatever their diversities, they all had this in common. They all felt that there was something lacking in their era which men who lived in other periods enjoyed; in particular, they regretted the absence of blood. The history of other times could boast of dynamic leaders who came to power through deeds of violence and through the full use of all the arts of persuasion, from bribery to torture, from poison to massacre. Such deeds they felt, were normal and healthy. In such an atmosphere culture must surely flourish. Was not the Italian Renaissance at once the most politically corrupt and culturally fertile era of modern times, they asked.

Yet how vapid were their own airs! A business civilization with all man's noble savagery stymied by commercial competition and election fights. Compare Gladstone to Nero, or Grover Cleveland to Caesare Borgia. The slaves had been liberated only to spread their slave morality throughout the world. There were long periods when the great powers were at peace with one another. When politicians arose to power, they talked, not of themselves, nor of the exhilaration of ruling, but rather of their willingness to serve the desires of the ignorant and the dull-witted.

We who live in a period of moral decline are, perhaps, not quite so enthusiastic as those who, like Moses, looked over into the Promised Land from a safe distance. For there always seems to be something bookish about prophets of animality. Although they held a fornicating, mass-trampling manhood in far greater esteem than the timid Victorian, they were none the less more secure, if less stimulated, in the company of the latter.

The same can be said of the modest and essentially ascetic men who heralded the dawn of a new era of sexual freedom— Ibsen, Samuel Butler, Bernard Shaw. How well would they survive in the Promised Land of orgy and promiscuity? When, at last, it came, when night-clubs and speakeasies were turned into brothels, and automobiles were turned into primordial caves, it was not altogether surprising that their spiritual descendants should retire from the Promised Land, Aldous Huxley into the ascetic cult of the Hindoos, and T. S. Eliot into the mysteries of the Church of England, or that novelists, as a whole, as if to emphasize their discomfort, should turn from the indulgences of the rich to the rough performances of sub-humans on the fringes of society, of slum-dwellers and sharecroppers.

And reality is even more uncomfortable for those who espoused animalism in politics. Oswald Spengler, for example, had the rare experience denied to his predecessor, Nietzsche. He survived to enter the Promised Land and to witness the rise of the Nazis. And he was outraged. Hitler, far from being the aristocratic hero that he had envisaged, was, he felt, a weak opportunist, who was as much a socialist as a nationalist, and who acted as a tool of the masses rather than as a genius who twisted and turned them to his own conceptions. Such were his impressions, before the purge of 1934, as recorded in *The Hour of Decision*. Needless to say, Spengler, once hailed as the theorist of Nazism, was sharply reprimanded and was retired in his declining years to the more modest study of animalism in classical antiquity.

Whatever the shortcomings of political life today, you cannot deny that it has blood. Our era has almost everything that an advocate of political animalism might wish— torture, violence, massacre, war, men strong and unscrupulous. And this animalism is in the service of both sides, of the revolutionaries in Italy, Germany and Spain, and of the revolutionaries in Russia. And yet, those who revel philosophically in this state of affairs apparently prefer to do so in other countries where political life is not yet so stimulating. And they seem to revel all the more merrily here in the United States, 4000 miles away from the Promised Lands.

For now that the dams are down and human animals rove the hinterland of Europe, there is so much brutishness in the new order that the Good Life cannot be lived under its rules. Those who felt that man's character would be enlarged by the opening of these new organs have been disappointed. In watching the spectacle the moral thinker is all too likely to turn sour and accept the European experiments as proof of the complete depravity of the human race.

6. SECOND WORLD WAR

The collapse of moral values has been so great since the First World War that it seems unlikely that the Second World War can make any further contribution. When the Germans marched into Poland, there was little of that surprise and moral outrage that accompanied their march into Belgium in 1914. The lamps of Europe did not suddenly go out, for they were already out in the areas concerned, and were burning low in England and France. Nobody had illusions that if only peace were maintained, culture, democracy, and mankind would prosper. The twentieth century no longer loomed ahead as a duplication on an even vaster scale of the nineteenth. It now had very definite and depressing characteristics of its own; and in looking forward, we were probably too pessimistic rather than the opposite.

Just as we had given ourselves up to angelic day-dreams on the eve of the First World War, so now we torture ourselves with animalic nightmares of equal extravagance. The Fascists have been teaching the philosophy of the total war, with war as the natural state of affairs, broken only by abnormal interludes of peace. During the past decade they have been aggrandizing themselves over the weak and vulnerable nations. In contemplating the possibility of the whole world in conflict, we naturally gave our imaginations free rein and felt that the end of civilization was at hand. But for all the fury of the German westward thrust, we are denied such drama. Instead of a sudden cataclysm, we face slow, unending vistas of destruction; and we await our turn to fight in a grim atmosphere. To date, the Second World War has added very little to a further decline in values. We have witnessed no barbarity that we had not already seen. The dissemination of strife, prejudice, and defeatism in enemy nations, the paralysis of the victim by bribery and cold terror, the exploitation of discontented elements, and then the final swoop—all these techniques of Fascist attack had been demonstrated before the outbreak of the Second World War. The only novelty lay in certain military practices, the use of parachute troops, dive bombers and tanks. These techniques applied on a vast scale and with startling efficiency overwhelmed the French Republic —not by the moral shock, but by the physical.

In this book I shall discuss the degree to which American ideals, particularly progressive ideals, have been affected by this world-wide deflation of values. We have felt the direct impact of the rise of Fascism in Europe. But that is only part of the story. Though in a milder way, we have been through many of the same experiences as have the Fascist countries: the First World War, declining foreign markets, economic stagnation.

When I describe the deflation of American ideals, I do not imply that we are doomed to the decadence of the Nazis. We are on our way down, but it is a partial and necessary descent. The fault with Nazism lies, not in its appeal to animalism, but to the wrong facets of animalism, to our proclivities that are most easily aroused and most destructive, such as the desire for dominating and intimidating other people. Democracy, deflated to its lowest terms, appeals to other proclivities, to tendencies which make for better social living, such as the desire for food and well-being. American ideals are being deflated like overblown bags; and as the process goes on, I believe we shall be all the stronger for the conflict that is at hand.

CHAPTER TWO

The Flight of the Angels

1. Progressive America
2. The Deflation of American Ideals
3. Self-Portrait of A Progressive
4. Have We Deflated Enough?

I. PROGRESSIVE AMERICA

THE issue of aristocracy vs. democracy has presented itself at many great crises in our history, and every time, the outcome has been uncertain. And yet, as the years laid to rest the contestants and the bitterness subsided, the champions of democracy emerge as true Americans and survive in our gallery of immortals, while the champions of aristocracy go down as un-American, and their reputations have, for the most part, crumbled like figures of clay.

Why is this? There is nothing inherently heroic about the democratic cause that recommends its devotees to immortality. Rather, I believe, it is because that cause has been slowly but surely winning. It had been gaining prestige from the French Revolution down to the First World War. In large measure we respect the names of Jefferson, Jackson, and Lincoln, not because they had glorious dreams, but because they sought to fulfill their dreams on the winning side.

I am convinced that if we had moved backward over these 150 odd years instead of forward, if we had moved from such democracy as we have achieved back to a planter and mercantile aristocracy, we would have had no hesitation in canonizing the other side. Our immortals would then be William Howard Taft, William McKinley, Jefferson Davis, John C. Calhoun, Nicholas Biddle, and Benedict Arnold. They would have been the great visionaries in the return to medievalism.

As it has turned out, however, time has been favorable to the course of increasing democratization, to the liberal or, as I prefer to call it, the progressive side. In fact we accept the achievements of a dynamic democracy without question and have almost forgotten that any other philosophy has ever flourished. Yet the Federalists once argued for a paternalistic government controlled by a commercial elite with the people restrained as a "great beast." Calhoun once defended the slave system of the ante-bellum South as a kind of Greek democracy. And at the close of the nineteenth century many Old Guard Republicans spoke openly for the rule of the fittest—the fittest being those who had survived in industrial competition. As in England the Whigs survived to write British history, so in America the progressives have survived to write ours. Today our conservatives have been sufficiently impressed by these developments that they no longer assert their aristocratic inclinations in such bold terms.

But if progressivism has triumphed according to this formula, that is no guaranty as to its future. The events in Europe have put progress itself in doubt. We can no longer be confident that in democratizing our economy the cost in liberties will be worth the gain in well-being. What we thought were contributions to progress may well be the fatal steps to a Fascist or Communist despotism. Perhaps there is a hump in the road and we have progressed as far as we can go without descending again.

With such uncertain conditions, all manner of men have come forth and challenged the President's reputation as a true progressive and a true American. Any public figure who stands virtually still no matter what the temptation will have his future reputation guaranteed by such prophets as *The New York Times* and by the other once-liberal organs. These papers stood bond for Burton Wheeler, Carter Glass, Edward Burke, John Garner, and Bennett Clark, who opposed the President's Court Plan. These men, they said, were in the great American tradition, and their names would some day glisten beside those of Patrick Henry and Sam Adams as the defenders of American liberties.

Never before could men stand pat with more assurance. In the days of the agrarian revolt and railroad legislation, conservatives opposed the progressive stream with direful warnings of disaster and dictatorship. In those days their prophecies were based on imagination. Now we have actually seen the implications of some of our measures in the terrible outlines of European despotism. The opposition, therefore, has become more credible and powerful than ever. Moreover, the recession of 1937, the elections of 1938, and the war in Europe have dampened and diverted the energies of reform. At each successive frustration the opposition has rejoiced only to awaken suddenly to the realization that the war crisis had saddled them with a third Roosevelt administration, and that, although the progressive could no longer attempt progress at home, he could still serve, and serve supremely, in the cause of democratic survival among the nations.

2. THE DEFLATION OF AMERICAN IDEALS

We progressives are, on the whole, very unstable people. As reformers, we are engaged in a task of limitless dimensions. There are endless wrongs to right, and beyond them, still other wrongs and still other tasks. Yet we persist in our visions of a "good society." We still believe that it is possible to establish justice as the ruling principle among men and we are as impatient as ever with small and immediate objectives.

But the very range of our ambition has been our undoing. It has led us away from the necessary and often unpleasant struggles of the day to tilting with impossible issues. Challenges open on every side, and our imaginations have wandered afield. Instead of staying at home and doing something to relieve our dependents, we have gone off to save distant and unknown maidens from obscure oppressors. We are distraught and often ineffectual. Don Quixote, in his attack upon the windmill, is our very arch-type.

Like every political writer, I am for good and against evil. But I must confess at the outset that I am more worried over the befuddlement of the forces of good than I am over the power of the forces of evil. I believe that in the struggle for progressive ideals we have lost more battles in our own camp than we have in open engagements with the enemy. I am not shocked by the existence of wrong and injustice and the resulting conflicts among men. What shocks me is the absurd baggage that we good people carry along with us only to clutter up the battlefield. It is no accident that satirists throughout the ages have spent their arsenal, not on obvious scoundrels like thieves, murderers, and tyrants, but on the comparatively well-meaning—on preachers, dreamers, intellectuals, moralists, doctors and lawyers, and now, most pertinently, progressives. For these invariably cut the most ridiculous figure.

It is my contention that now, at last, we progressives are a formidable force, because we have dropped our excess baggage by the wayside. To be sure, we have not done this as a conscious feat of ideological strategy, but rather through the force of circumstances. The world simply became so hostile that we could not afford to tilt at windmills. We were backed against the wall and forced to fight for our lives. Such a circumstance, indeed, seems to be the only one under which we can channel our energies for a single immediate purpose. If ever the tension is relaxed, we shall probably bound off again in the old futile and unstable manner.

There are many people who regret this forcible concentration of progressive energies and the dropping of excess baggage. They demand that we restore our spiritual objectives alongside our economic and political. Let me reassure them on this point. We are really far better off where we are, and the rigors of war, depression, and Fascism are all for the best. I shall illustrate this by a brief historical account of progressive idealism in America.

Those who fought the American Revolution as well as the generation that followed were, on the whole, realistic and hard-fisted men, with a clear understanding of what they were fighting for and what they were fighting against. Their energies were expended upon efforts to establish and invigorate the institutions of the feeble Republic. From Samuel Adams to Andrew Jackson, they learned their progressivism in a school of violence and they breathed their ideals in the enlightened air of eighteenth century rationalism.

Later in the nineteenth century, however, the progressives, unchastened by any prolonged economic impasse, and with only the sporadic crises of the slavery conflict to bring them down to earth, expanded their program over space and time. They took upon themselves vast projects in spiritual engineering. They conjured out of their imaginations burdens that would strain a man as strong as Hercules and as high-minded as Zeus. There was, for example, a great liberal renaissance in New England in the 1840's and 1850's. It was not only political and economic, but religious and ethical as well, nourished on the blouzy romantic winds of transcendentalism blowing in from Germany. Indeed, it was characteristic of this golden age that it was concerned with everybody's problems but its own.

There can be little doubt that slavery was the one vital issue in those days, particularly as it was involved in the admission of new states and the sectional balance of power in the country. Yet the very people who were most uncompromising towards slavery were people like William Lloyd Garrison and the New England Abolitionists who had the least contact with its evils and who had the smallest stake in its abolition. Instead of collectivizing the real world, the Utopians of Brook Farm, George Ripley and Theodore Parker, set out to collectivize a private little world of their own. John Humphrey Noyes founded a cult which placed spiritual perfection above the demands of civil society. Generally the reformers of that day scattered from the main road into the forest of pacifism, prohibition, anarchism, prison reform, and vegetarianism.

After the doldrums of the Reconstruction Period following the Civil War, we entered a new golden age of reform, which lasted from the turn of the century down to the First World War and which Claude Bowers has called the Progressive Era. Here again we find a confusion of purposes, a vast proliferation of good causes with Christian and Puritan ideals mixed in with political ones. Here again the reformers who attempted to clean out the Augean stables of the American city were as much concerned with saloons and houses of ill-fame as they were with traction franchises. And those who attempted to repair the depredations of our great industrial barons were likewise distraught, laboring to salvage the pocketbook of the underdog by first salvaging his soul.

Thus, the progressive ideal had expanded to a dangerous point on the very eve of the explosion. In 1910 William Allen White had written:

> "The most hopeful sign of the times lies in the fact that the current is almost world-wide. The same striving to lift men to higher things, to fuller enjoyment of the fruits of our civilization, to a wider participation in the blessings of modern society—in short, to 'a more abundant life'—a movement which indicates that in the soul of the people there is a conviction of their past unrighteousness."[1]

It is often said that the Anglo-Saxon countries are practical and have no patience with the philosophical theorizing of the continent. It seems to me that, however practical we are in business or in professional politics, we are far from practical in things of less immediate concern—like the endeavor to improve the community. The various progressive cults that have flourished and gained followings in America have been as weird as Byzantine curiosities.

Yet somehow, despite our vagaries, we have managed to get things done. We freed the slaves in the Civil War. In the Progressive Era we further democratized our political machinery and made beginnings in industrial regulation. In the disillusion of 1920 Oswald Garrison Villard wrote that we were then no further along the road than we were in 1900.[2] If he was talking about the ethical improvement of the human stock, then he was certainly right. But if he was talking about political and economic reforms, he was wrong. For however befuddled the progressive movement had been, it did bequeath institutional changes for future generations; and if there had not been that confusion of objectives which Villard still manifests, there is no telling how far progressivism might have gone.

In the life-time of those now middle-aged, our progressive

ideals have been deflated; and it is the history of this deflation from the last flowering of nineteenth century idealism in the Progressive Era to the bald and realistic objectives of the New Deal that I am attempting to record.

First of all, the progressive movement no longer feels that it is moving toward the millenium. It is now harnessed to the business cycle, and starts and stops according to the demands of recovery. Protests have been voiced in the past during other depressions, and reforms have resulted which were compounded out of odd bits of monetary and fiscal folklore. Only now for the first time have the progressives discovered the best economic wisdom which is also the most politically expedient. In New Deal theory the progressive ideal has been changed from a race horse into a mule, whose value lies, not in its beauty and morality, but in its practical usefulness in a world of hard economics.

Secondly, the ethical-religious objectives have been dropped from political-economic objectives. With the repeal of Prohibition, sin was returned to the jurisdiction of the churches where it belongs, and the present administration has shown little inclination to reclaim it. President Roosevelt has his hands full with other problems.

Thirdly, since the rise of large-scale capitalism, we progressives can no longer devote ourselves to destroying the trusts. We can no longer be merely dragon-killers. We have come to depend so much on the dragon that we would be lost without his services. The problem now is to domesticate him; to put him in harness and ride him about the countryside. We need the ability to manage rather than to destroy. And we can no longer think that we will be free once we have destroyed capitalism; such destruction is no longer practical. We must get used to huge corporations and great concentrations of power, but now we must learn to control them for popular ends.

Many people have observed this, most articulately the

opponents of the New Deal. We find much of this deflation described in a campaign speech of Herbert Hoover,
albeit with somewhat less sympathy than I have displayed
here.

> "There are already five evil products from these years of the
> New Deal that have become self-evident.
> "The first is the degeneration of political morals to the lowest
> ebb in our history.
> "The second is the malignant growth of personal power in this
> Republic.
> "The third is the heart-breaking growth of hate, class division,
> and disunity in the most classless country in the world.
> "The fourth is that underneath all this is a creeping collect-
> ivism that is steadily eating away the vitalities of free enter-
> prise.
> "The fifth is that after six years of these policies we have eleven
> million people out of jobs. . . . ."[3]

But the energies of the progressive movement have been
affected even more by the tensions of the modern world.
Since the beginning of the Second World War they have
been twisted from their normal channels of domestic reform
and applied to the defence of the nation. Fascism, con-
veyed by the planes and tanks of the German war machine,
has smashed French democracy and won domination of the
continent. We, in this country, can no longer afford the
luxury of improving our institutions.

Wilson's New Freedom was also brought to a close by the
menace of foreign autocracy, by the imperial ambitions of
Kaiser Wilhelm. Here again, the tensions that shape our
ideals today are much greater and much more terrible than
those of the past. While Wilson shifted from concerns at
home to concerns abroad under a cloud of international
aspirations, demanding the League of Nations and Fourteen
Points, we are shifting under the hard necessity of saving
our skins; and we have had less demand for grandiose

schemes of world-wide reconstruction. Even before the collapse of France world changes were affecting the nature of progressive idealism. We had been subjected to a series of shocks from the Versailles Treaty to the Soviet-Nazi Pact; and we have been drifting in the direction of autarchy through the contraction of our foreign markets.

3. SELF-PORTRAIT OF A PROGRESSIVE

Thus the contemporary progressives are very circumscribed. Soviet Russia has explored the road ahead of us into socialism, and the prospects are now neither so vague nor so thoroughly pleasant as they were in blue-print. Nazi Germany has loomed up on our ideological rear; and we are conscious how fragile are even such gains as we have made. We no longer project our reforms into an infinity of time. The future is like the Gorgon head, too horrible to look upon. It is little wonder that we do little thinking about it. We cannot see much beyond the next few months, nor imagine very clearly any settlement of the Second World War except a catastrophic one.

The progressive movement has been operating on a short-run basis, balancing the books each year, delighted with such paltry profits as have been made, and planning ahead only as far as the next session of Congress. The American Civil Liberties Union, for example, publishes each summer an account of violations of civil rights, and they make their judgments in terms of the preceding years, hardly mentioning the shadows which threaten. In this warped and frantic period we have our ups and downs and we hold parades in the light of momentary successes. Indeed, the present has been so much more real than the future that we have no qualms about gaining these successes on the providence of future taxpayers. Hence the paradox of an inflated national debt arising out of deflated national idealism.

Even the totalitarian nations that are responsible for the foreshortening of our vision have themselves been subject to the same urgency. Programs that would have formerly stretched into the millenium have been condensed into the Five Year Plan in Soviet Russia, and into a Four Year Plan in Nazi Germany.

With the loss of assurance about the millenium, we are free of another of our failings. We are no longer perfectionists. There was a time when we confronted our statesmen with pictures of ideal societies or with patterns of the ideal conduct necessary to the achievement of that society. In the Progressive Era, for example, we demanded of our public men an integrity that should have been applied only to clergymen or to college presidents. When we ended up with Woodrow Wilson, who was a little of both, it served us right.

In the main line of socialist thought all policies are inevitably judged in the light of rigid Marxist doctrine. The progressives who had acquired strong socialist leanings in the period after the First World War were merciless in their first reception of the New Deal. Why, they asked, had not the President nationalized the banks, taken over the railroads, and solved the crisis by abolishing the profit system? Gradually, as the precariousness of the New Deal and, indeed, of all democracy, became clear, they grew less exacting in their demands. In fact they grew so completely pragmatic and so completely loyal to the Roosevelt leadership that, in domestic policy at least, there was, for a while, virtually no opposition on the left.

The real perfectionists were the conservatives. They not only had a perfectionist feeling for what was good, namely, private enterprise, but also credited the New Deal with a kind of negative perfectionism in what was evil, "Communism" and "Fascism." The conservatives are now the dreamers and the Utopians. Stuart Chase and Thurman Arnold, among others, have made great reputations by mocking the cries of "Fascism," "Communism," and" Un-Americanism" uttered in opposition to the engineering feats of the New Deal. It seems that the side with a real mission comes down to earth and talks horse sense, while the opposition is frantic and perfectionist. And I am thankful indeed that at last it is the turn of the progressives to be hard-boiled.

Along with our failings of optimism and perfectionism, we progressives also had a tendency to righteousness. Indeed I do not think I could have been a progressive at any other time than the present. I do not think I could have espoused any of our various causes since the American Revolution or at least since the election of Andrew Jackson with much enthusiasm. I am no St. George. I am not the sort of person who goes out slaying dragons, supremely confident that I am thereby ridding my fellows of a great menace. I am not convinced that human integrity will be restored once the dragons of everyday life are removed. If we are to fight oppression, we ought to fight with full knowledge of our own limitations. We have no need to assume poses of self-righteousness and moral superiority. We progressives are simply one kind of animal engaged in a struggle with other animals, dragons or capitalists, as the case may be. Instead of being superior to our enemies, we are probably worse because we have been oppressed and defrauded by them. And we must show our worth in the only sense in which the word has meaning—by developing superior strength and skill in combat. Nor do I believe that the heroic attitude is either necessary or appropriate. We do not have to meet the dragon face to face. We do not have to approach him in a public encounter when he may be much more vulnerable in the privacy of his domestic life. I, for example, would not hesitate, where possible, to stir dissention within the dragonian family, or perhaps simply divert the menace by substituting some more innocuous diet for the present *table d'hôte* of maids, widows, and orphans. Let us not be deceived. The progressive struggle is simply the struggle between the animals who are best adapted to the future and the animals who were best adapted to the past. Nor is it any more glorious in itself in the social setting than when viewed as the survival of the fittest in the jungle.

Oswald Garrison Villard has written that we progressives have always had "the rightful consciousness that the angels have fought with us." That was precisely our shortcoming, and we can now rejoice that we are rid of such allies. For the presence of angels in the progressive ranks was certainly embarrassing, at least to rough souls like myself. Even in such bitter conflict as that involving social reconstruction, certain rules of combat should be observed. There should be an understanding with the enemy to fight on essentially the same level and over essentially the same issues. There should be no sudden intervention of Higher Powers.

The angels handicapped us at the start. We were assured that the moral order rendered our victory inevitable, and with this assurance we became condescending. We could afford to be patient with the villain in the first act because we knew that he would be disposed of before the final curtain. In this way we did the capitalists a great injustice. We made them feel ashamed of their greed, only to appropriate it later for ourselves. Moreover, we have tended to underestimate their powers. Villains without souls and without the aid of angels would seem to be very weak; for whatever their worldly successes, they would seem to be without basic integrity. This has proved an unwarranted judgment. We have been hacking away at them at least since the turn of the century and they are still going strong.

4. HAVE WE DEFLATED ENOUGH?

While there has been considerable deflation of American progressivism we have not yet hit the bottom. No matter how attractively we wrap our packages and how reasonably we set the price in the market place of political ideas, the reaction always seems to supply gaudier wrappings and to be able to undersell us. Throughout the great days of the New Deal unscrupulous adventurers have drummed up a bootleg trade on the side—Huey Long, Dr. Townsend, Father Coughlin, Martin Dies. And some day they may well flood our politics with their rottenness and drive the progressive ideal from the market place.

Political fights, for the most part, end up on the lowest common denominator between the two sides. But in this case there are difficulties. For when the deflated progressive cause was winning great victories with the New Deal the conservative cause was virtually bankrupt. For eight years the Republicans have groomed one doughty challenger after another—Hoover, Landon, and Willkie. But they could never endow them with an issue more potent than opposition to or imitation of the New Deal. In the elections of 1938 this carping strategy began to take effect; but the general satisfaction over the President's conduct of foreign policy in the ensuing years was so great that in the elections of 1940 the Republicans failed again. In desperation they had sent out an investigation committee to discover an attractive program. In the nature of the case it was doomed. The Republicans could not possibly meet the deflation of the New Deal with a deflation of their own. Whereas New Deal deflation exposed its bald attachment to the rights of the majority groups, Republican deflation simply exposed their bald attachment to the rights of Big Business, as in the Liberty League adventure.

And so it has come about that the most dangerous rivals in the market place have not been the conservatives, but rather the crackpot movements. In some cases, as with the Townsend Plan, these have been allied with the Republicans; in others, as with the Dies Committee, they have been associated with the anti-New Deal Democrats; and in the extreme case of the American Fascists, they have been endowed by independent and desperate industrialists and by foreign powers.

In every case there is the attempt to provide the masses with an even more glittering diversion than the New Deal. Look at the agitation for old age pensions, the Townsend Plan and the Ham and Eggs Plan in California. Here are promises of extravagant benefits to the "senior citizens," calculated to appeal to their stomachs and to their vanity, where they are most vulnerable. No legitimate progressive program can possibly compete on this level. For no responsible leader would arouse expectations which he could not possibly meet and which, even if he could, would grossly distort the government's expenditures for the benefit of a single voting bloc. These promoters are indeed insidious when they attempt to justify their plans, not on grounds of moral obligation, but with the same economic apologia as the New Deal—that is, priming the pump for prosperity.

Then, there is the Fascist and Anti-Semitic ideal which has been openly advocated by the conspiratorial Father Coughlin, in which the progressive aim has been twisted around in seductive and treacherous form. In some respects it harkens back to the old anti-trust agitation of the early 1900's. The progressives were then fighting the elite of the corporations, a minority which held the strategic posts of our economy. Now, say the Fascists, there is an even more dangerous elite that encompasses Big Business as well as all other imaginable evils, that is, the Jewish International, which exploits the people through its Jew-bankers, expropriates them through its Jew-Communists, and generally controls the papers they read and the politicians they vote for, and foments at will depressions, wars, revolutions.

Once the people are convinced of the existence of this new elite, it can be attacked much more easily than the old elite of Big Business. For the latter are fairly remote. You never see them, and should you venture to assault them in the seat of their power you are either bribed, defamed or arrested. Besides, your antagonism is likely to be blunted by a latent admiration.

Not so with the Jewish International. It manifests itself everywhere, not only among its wealthy representatives but also among its poor. It does not take much courage to swoop down on these humbler and more accessible members. Nor is there any question of latent admiration. Antagonism on economic grounds is augmented by antagonism on racial grounds, by vengeance on a socially-inferior people who seem to have risen to power.

Then there is the Dies Committee, which concentrates on the bogies of political life, the Communists and, to some extent, the Fascists. Here again we find a diversion from the progressive ideal which does not concern itself with the serious and difficult problem of curing American ills, but looks to the fringes of the political market place with all the unhealthy fascination of a lynching party. Nor was Mr. Dies satisfied with mere byplays. By 1938 he had moved by flank attacks from the bogies of the nether world to the more respectable and more potent bogies in and around the White House.

In the national emergency brought on by the German victories, the bogies have, to some extent, actually materialized. And we have tacitly admitted that what we thought was an imaginary menace is a real menace. This change of view has been accompanied by a change in terminology. Nazis, Fascist sympathizers, and Communists whom we once hounded for the advocacy of "Un-American" programs have turned into "Fifth Columnists" whom we now charge with undermining American sovereignty. Despite the increased importance of these bogies, public persecution of or antipathy to all aliens and dissident groups is no solution. The Fifth Column is within the jurisdiction of the police, and should be handled by them, not by the mob. Under the circumstances, progressives are making it their business to defend the nation with a minimum of hysteria and a maximum of civil liberty.

In the long run, I believe, foreign ideas, if not foreign agents, can be overcome in the competition of the marketplace. In recent years American ideals have been considerably toughened. We cannot cry that the pensioners are faithless or that the Fascists are intolerant. We ourselves are, perhaps, a little faithless in riding roughshod over campaign platforms, and no doubt a little intolerant of economic royalists. For we, like they, are fighting a battle with every means at our disposal. If we win it will not be through moral superiority, but because our program has greater vision and works better. After all, the New Deal has within bounds done infinitely better than its predecessor, while foreign systems have already revealed their full potentialities abroad. If the American people, aware of all this, are still deceived, then there is no hope. We cannot deflate democracy much further.

PART II

——— —

DEFLATION IN MORAL CONTENT

CHAPTER THREE

Progressive Ambitions: 1865-1912

1. The Search for An Ideal
2. The Mugwumps
3. The Agrarians
4. The Awakening to Evil
5. Attack on The Bosses
6. Trust-Busting

1. THE SEARCH FOR AN IDEAL

IN THE period between the end of the Civil War and 1900 the economic landscape of the United States changed. At the end of the Civil War America was predominantly agricultural and industry, for the most part, was in many small hands. Then a few men obtained great power over the manufacture of essential goods, such as steel, oil, anthracite coal, sugar and tobacco. They carved out great principalities in the American market and forced a toll on all who did business with them. Investment banks aided the process and soon found themselves in control of the very princes whom they were aiding. And they were called variously, "steel kings," "coal czars," "money moguls," and generally, "robber barons." Nor was this feudal reference unjust. For though the Constitution forbids the granting of titles, we had acquired an industrial and financial aristocracy that had all the qualifications.

New industries developed in the period after 1900—automobiles, radio, motion pictures, airplanes. Industries and banks that were already large grew larger. Yet from the point of view of economic institutions the main lines were already there. On the map of the American market the chief dukedoms and kingdoms were already sketched in. The same period had witnessed the founding of General Electric, International Harvester, and the American Telephone and Telegraph Company—and they still tower over their respective markets today, forty years later. The period of evolution, evolving new species and genera of economic institutions, was over. The Mesozoic Era of the 1870's to 1890's had passed. And the landscape, despite superficial changes, looks essentially the same now as it did then.

We progressives have been trying to extend democracy into this industrial feudal system. We have been trying for fifty years or more and have come no further than the New Deal. For we have been groping and fumbling by empirical contact with the system itself. We do not believe in changing society according to plan. We move from one logical step to another in slow ten-year strides. Meanwhile the socialist intellectual by a mental operation leaps over all these preliminaries. Confronted by evil, he makes a sweeping analysis as to effects and cause, and knowing the cause, he prescribes the cure.

Our pace has been so slow that many of the alert men who have grown up with the ideals of one phase of progressivism have become restless and dissatisfied and have gone on to seek ideals many jumps ahead. Lincoln Steffens is perhaps the most striking example. As one of the muckrakers, he helped to educate the American people to Theodore Roosevelt's Square Deal, but gradually he broke under its limitations and drifted off from the main stream. In 1908 he wrote a book setting forth a new kind of reform program for Boston, but could find no publisher. In his *Autobiography* he wrote of it:

"That book is a disappointment to everybody, and my theory
is that it had no relation to any kind of thinking that was being
done at that time.   It was an attempt to muckrake our American ideals (not our bad conduct but our virtues) as a sign and
a continuing cause of evil."[1]

Later Steffens went from a prematurely deflated progressivism that was very much in the spirit of what we have
today to downright Soviet Communism, which he extolled
with the flourish, "I have seen the future and it works."

We proceeded in our peculiar fashion, scorning both
European experience and European theory.   Nor could we
expect that the Founding Fathers would have been of much
help.   They could hardly have foreseen the economic
monstrosity that was to arise one hundred years after their
time, nor could they have written a philosophy sufficient
to deal with it.   The cry that has filled the air in recent
years, that we have been stealing European thunder, is
pretty hollow.   After floundering around with the problems of monopoly and finance capitalism all these years, it
would be a sad commentary on the American genius if we
could not at least claim the New Deal as our own.

Why has it taken so long?   At this distance, it is difficult
to recall the bewilderment and uncertainty that greeted the
emergence of monopoly capitalism.   Something new and
evil had come into American life; that was certain.   It
made itself felt in a variety of ways—through exorbitant
railroad rates and industrial prices, through corrupt legislatures, through increasingly violent depressions, and through
a slow realization of closing frontiers and diminishing
opportunity.   There were so many ramifications that the
progressives of the day could not see the picture as a whole.
"What is wrong with us?" they asked.   "Is it just some
passing corruption, or is it a permanent change in our way
of life?"   We sought the Achilles Heel of capitalism by

throwing javelins at every conceivable point in its anatomy —at corrupt politicians, at legislatures, at railroads, industrial trusts and at Wall Street.   By hit or miss, we slowly broadened our vision and sharpened our weapons.

And here is the paradox that while we have increased our devices and moved on from individualist to collectivist solutions, we have done so only at the cost of deflating our ideals. For the more we advance in economic sophistication, the more we lose in moral sophistication.   We have become effective in dealing with monopoly capitalism only by loosening our standards of personal integrity and inventing new standards of social organization, cold and analytical.

To begin with we felt that the evil in society was merely an occasional corruption of wicked men in political and business life.   Then in the period from the agrarian revolts of the Greenbackers to Wilson's "New Freedom," there was a slow realization that evil was somehow deeply-rooted and that even if all men were angels, we would still pay exorbitant rates and prices.   We came to demand less and less from individuals and more and more from institutions. We withdrew human character from the range of our reforms.   Politics, in this way, became dehumanized.   Nor has the process been confined to politics.   It has appeared wherever men sought a remote explanation for the causes of behaviour—like the attitude of criminologists who blame not the criminal but his environment and that of critics who credit not the artist, but his economic conditioning and his libidinous sub-conscious.

This attitude may make for sweeping reforms, but at the same time it makes for greater indifference as to the individual.   Men were once believed to be the masters of their fate and they were held responsible for their actions. When they became demented or turned criminal, we locked them up.   When they did something noble we crowned them with olive wreaths. Everybody was expected to become angelic, to represent the noblest part of his heritage and his aspirations, and whoever lapsed back towards the animal, whether in greed or sensuality, had to pay the penalty.

Much of this has changed. We do not expect individuals to find their own way to heaven. We pass laws and create institutions that force them to go to heaven whether they want to or not. It is not remarkable any more when politicians or corporations act with restraint, for our institutions have so developed that it would be unprofitable to do otherwise. A politician, for example, can no longer buy a seat in the Senate as easily as before the ratification of the Seventeenth Amendment, nor can an industrial firm cut wages quite so drastically as in the days before the C. I. O. began its organizing drive.

Woodrow Wilson's New Freedom represents a mid-point in the movement from the moral approach to the engineering approach. Wilson saw the evil in society as something more intangible and yet far more encompassing than the bugaboos of Theodore Roosevelt. Yet despite the range of his vision it lacked concreteness. It remained for the New Deal to find more exact objectives in social engineering. Wilson's vague and happy optimism on the progressive side was largely a reflection of capitalist optimism on the conservative side. In a period of capitalist desperation the second Roosevelt has had to apply his progressivism to very definite problems. He has had to harness his New Deal to the business cycle in an effort to restore the national income. As a result, the progressive cause has found purpose at the cost of its spiritual content.

This broadening scope of engineering projects and decreasing concern for the moralities has appeared on the moving front of the progressive struggle. In these three chapters I have traced its development in national politics since the Civil War, but I have not found any comparable development in state politics. As major reforms increasingly become functions of the federal government, local government has been removed from the scene of action. Thus disputes over the integrity of candidates in Massachusetts, Indiana or Illinois today manifest the same heat and futility that they did in the nation at large at the time of Grover Cleveland.

2. THE MUGWUMPS

The name "Mugwump" was first used to brand the Independent Republicans who refused to support Blaine in 1884. But it has come to apply to that whole genus of civil service reformers and free traders who rose in protest against the first Grant administration, continued to flourish more or less until the Bryan campaign in 1896 and who declined in the uncongenial airs of McKinley imperialism and Theodore Rooseveltian progressivism. They included in their ranks such gifted writers and reformers as E. L. Godkin, George William Curtis, Carl Schurz, occasionally the young T. R., Henry Cabot Lodge and Henry Adams, and they claimed as their champions Presidents Rutherford B. Hayes and Grover Cleveland.

The Mugwumps were not progressives in their historical context: they did not attempt to extend democracy into monopoly capitalism. They were not looking for new devices with which to meet altered circumstances. They did not have to grope for an ideal. They had one ready made from England—the liberalism of free enterprise. And in the attempt to apply this ideal over here, it was soon apparent that their "Good Society" existed more in the past than in the future.

Being outmoded at the start, their program was characterized by high moral indignation and futility—veritable marks of bankruptcy. Monopolies, they said, had been created by corrupt public officials who sold out the principles of free trade and raised the tariff under the bribes of corporations. If the farmers and trade unions met this situation by organizing and bribing the officials for their own ends, the situation would become even worse. Irreparable damage had already been done in the protected industries, and our only hope for the future lay in the selection of officials of such high moral stature or with such institutional restraints that they could really resist all further temptation.

During this period a reputation for integrity became the greatest asset a public figure could have. When old Charles Sumner died, Carl Schurz said of him that "He was always in morals while in politics. He never was anything but a Senator with a conscience",[2] which was very high praise indeed from a Mugwump. And of President Hayes, under whom he served as Secretary of the Interior, Schurz wrote in similar vein:

> "The uprightness of his character and the exquisite purity of his life, public as well as domestic, exercised a conspicuously wholesome influence not only upon the *personnel* of the governmental machinery, but also upon the social atmosphere of the national capital while he occupied the White House."[3]

And the Mugwumps were perfectly consistent in their attitude towards Grover Cleveland, when his enemies charged that, for all his spotlessness in public life, he nonetheless had committed an indiscretion in private life which burdened him with an illegitimate child. For they felt it was far worse to rob the public treasury than to commit a private sin. And they cherished a man who could refrain from the former, even though he lapsed into the latter.

The Mugwumps made protest against the Jacksonian

"spoils system."   Democracy may be all right, they argued, as a system of government, but it was hardly a principle for the recruitment of our public officials.   "Public office," said Cleveland, "is a public trust"; and presumably only men endowed with disembodied purity and restraint could fill the requirements.   They advocated a kind of moral aristocracy, the rule of the "best people."

Although they lived through some of the most flagrant political corruption in our history, the Mugwumps did not lose faith in the possibilities of a political party.   When the Republican Party with which they had been closely associated in the slavery controversy had fulfilled its high mission and settled down to the boodle of the Grant administration, they decided to break away and form a Liberal Republican Party, to corral the "better elements" of both parties in support of a new ideal.   Somehow at their convention in 1872 professional politicians outmanoeuvered the Mugwumps and secured the nomination of Horace Greeley over their favorite, Charles Francis Adams.

To men of principle this was grievous indeed.   Greeley, despite his popularity with labor, was an advocate of high tariff, and the Mugwumps of course were free traders. Although they supported Greeley, they did so in a desultory and half-hearted manner.   Carl Schurz in a letter to a friend lamented that the whole Liberal Republican movement had been "dragged down to the level of an ordinary political operation" and that it had been betrayed by "a combination of politicians striking and executing a bargain in the open light of day."[4]

In their individual reforms they were more successful. Every Democratic platform since 1872 had promised some kind of civil service reform.   In 1882, after a series of scandals in the Republican administration, including the star route frauds and the murder of President Garfield, the Democrats came to power in Congress. Driven by an avenging tide, President Arthur supported what became the Pendleton Act, setting up the Civil Service Commission. In the first year 13,000 jobs were put in the classified service. The number increased under Cleveland who, for all his fine talk, still dispensed a goodly number of jobs to the bosses.

Ballot reform was another special triumph for Mugwumpery. Here too there had been flagrant abuses which shocked the public conscience. In most states at this time the election machinery was extra-legal. Abuse was easy; and when a series of national elections was so close that the election of a President depended on a corrupt organization in Indiana or New York, there came the inevitable protest. Mugwump publications like *The Century* argued for the Australian system, whereby the ballot was supplied by the state and the procedure was secret. In 1888 Massachusetts was the first state to introduce ballot reform, and ten years later all the states had followed suit.

In so far as the Mugwumps effected institutional reforms and contributed to the development of more efficient government their work was not in vain. But in their emphasis on moral character they were misjudging the nature of governmental problems. And indeed they implanted this emphasis so deeply into the progressive tradition that we have been distracted by it ever since. Such a political program made the greatest demands on its following. When a Mugwump strutted into high office and assumed an angelic pose, he may have done more than justice to the human race, but he was incapable of performing the ignoble work that arises from the fact that mankind has animal needs as well as angelic. As a result, Mugwump officials rarely lasted more than one term.

3. THE AGRARIANS

In the normal course of expansion after the Civil War the submerged economic groups were not given to reflection upon their plight in society nor did they question social and political institutions. Momentum swept them along in unresisting ignorance, and prosperity supplied a kind of occupational therapy for discontent. As long as crops were good and the frontier expanding they did not disparage the great railroad fortunes. They were not outraged by the corruption of their parties and legislatures.

Periodically between the Civil War and the end of the McKinley prosperity there were panics and years of depression. Suddenly the submerged groups were brought up sharp against an impasse; despite the American promise of equal and limitless opportunity, they were trapped in their stations. Each time they tried to take stock of the forces in the economy and to secure relief. In the panic of 1873 the farmers attacked the debt structure and the domination of the railroads. In 1884 they repeated these strictures and were joined by the urban workers who had their own ax to grind against monopoly in general and against the unlimited immigration that was ruining the labor market. And again these groups were heard in the agitation that began with falling prices in 1889 and culminated in the panic of 1893. In each instance a third party arose to articulate the protest. The party usually lasted four or five years and then disappeared with the return of prosperity. This agrarian pressure was largely responsible for the setting up of the Interstate Commerce Commission in 1887 and for the passage of the Sherman Anti-Trust Act in 1890, but these were bi-partisan measures, and in general, they failed to create much of a legislative stir on the federal plane.

Nonetheless, the agrarian leaders whipped up a fury of

almost revolutionary energy which survived the McKinley prosperity and gave momentum to the Progressive Era. In the Populist Party they twisted the resentment of the Southern agrarian away from the Yankees and the carpet-baggers and poured it into more fruitful channels, against the new monster of industrial combination that was trans-forming the new South as well as the North; and they united this rebel contingent with the Knights of Labor and the western farmers. They brought to the national scene a program that was to continue to have an effective appeal for the next twenty-five years, including such things as, abolition of landlords, initiative and referendum, direct election of Senators, the eight-hour day, postal savings bank, a graduated income tax, an additional currency to be lent at low interest rates, and the government ownership of railroads, telegraph, and telephone.

But, as William Allen White said, it was not until this "clamor" had been transformed into "sentiment" that the reforms were brought up for legislative action. The fiery figures of the agrarian movement, Tom Watson, Ignatius Donnelly, "Sockless" Jerry Simpson, gave way to the more astute Bryan and he, in turn, to the more urbane Theodore Roosevelt and Woodrow Wilson. Through these shifts in leadership each leader felt that his successor was stealing his thunder, and slowly the Populist Party died, not in futility, but rendered obsolete by more successful agencies.

Perhaps the main reason why the agrarians failed to make headway at this time was that they spent so much energy on cheap money—in the Greenback movement and in the movement for the free coinage of silver. This became the great obsession, the panacea. It was much easier than institutional reforms. It was easier to understand and more automatic in its operations. It diverted the attention of the agrarians from the difficult business of progressivism to an over-night Utopia.

What would have happened if William Jennings Bryan had been elected in 1896? Obviously a devaluation of the currency would have eased some of the debt burden. But as a cure-all for the ailments of our economy it would not have gone very deep. It amounted to a handout, and that is the simplest demand that could be made on the government. It required little reflection—little inquiry into the evil in the economic system that had caused the impasse and little ingenuity for dealing with that evil. Its appeal lay in a simple idea: when the all-providing economy fails to provide one looks to government to supply what is missing. Government then becomes a supplement to the normal sources of income. The handout program of protest still persists today in the form of lavish old-age pensions and social credit schemes.

The Populists were fully aware of these shortcomings. At the Populist convention of 1896 one faction accurately foretold the doom that would come by abandoning a thoroughgoing reform program for the Pied Piper of free silver. By throwing its lot with Bryan, the Democratic candidate, the Populist Party went into decline, and after lingering on for a few elections, finally disappeared. Henry Demarest Lloyd wrote *in memoriam*:

> "The free silver movement is a fake. Free silver is the cowbird of the reform movement. It waited until the nest had been built by the sacrifices and labors of others and then it laid its eggs in it, pushing out the others which lie smashed on the ground."[5]

Bryan of course was defeated. The McKinley prosperity soon arrived and, leavened by the Alaska gold rush, brought on the same inflation and high prices that the agrarians had been shouting for all those years. The agrarians had unquestionably been aware of the evil in society. But, for the most part, they were vague as to its nature. They were not yet fully awake to the vast change that the corporations had wrought in the American scene.

4. THE AWAKENING TO EVIL

When the awakening finally arrived it was spectacular. It was characterized by a sudden enthusiasm for information about the new industrial feudalism. Muckrakers multiplied and flourished. They had been purveying their wares a number of years before, in such works as *Wealth and Commonwealth* by Henry Demarest Lloyd. Now they had their hey-day in the periods from 1903 to 1906 and from 1909 to 1911.[6] Magazines like *McClure's*, *Collier's*, and *Hampton's* with exposés of almost every conceivable evil in public life achieved circulations varying from a half million to over a million. Most shocking of all were Ida M. Tarbell's revelations of the devious Standard Oil Company, Tom Lawson's inside stories of Wall Street, Lincoln Steffens' *The Shame of the Cities* and Upton Sinclair's novel on the packing houses, *The Jungle*.

The muckrakers, however, were no more sophisticated about their revelations than their readers. For them too it was a sudden awakening to the evil in their midst. They had neither anticipated it, nor could they predict where it would lead. They expressed a kind of adolescent bewilderment. They were both shocked at the dimensions of the marauding and fascinated by its cynicism and ruthlessness. Like youth discovering the adult world of sex and its evils, they were discovering the world of adult capitalism and its evils.

Eventually, of course, as Upton Sinclair reveals in *The Brass Check*, the monster brought pressure on the magazines

to restrain their forays. This taught the muckrakers a
lesson: that the evil had wider ramifications throughout our
institutions than they had supposed and that anti-capitalist
investigation could not be dabbled in for its sheer fascination. But at first they were quite unsuspecting—both the
muckrakers and the muckraked. They were unaware that
all this was dynamite spread abroad among the reading
public. Here was a charming spectacle that would be seen
no more—an important sector of the public press playing a
more progressive role than a progressive administration and,
on occasion, forcing the administration's hand.

Hampton's Magazine expressed the spirit of the muckrakers in their statement of purpose: "We are going to
expose evil wherever we can; we are going to expose it calmly
and truly; we are going to expose it in order that it may be
replaced by good." Frederick C. Howe in his *Confessions
of a Reformer*, written years later, comments on the naïveté
of this simple faith. The progressives, he says, thought it
sufficient to make people see what was wrong; they did not
realize that the mind "refused to work against economic
interests." On the other hand, Ray Stannard Baker argued
that if they had taken a stronger stand their ideas would
never have been accepted—indeed, that their very strength
was derived from not prescribing remedies for the evils
they depicted. Certainly only a few went as far as socialism—notably Upton Sinclair, Charles Edward Russell,
and after years of groping, Lincoln Steffens. William Archer
in *The American Cheap Magazine* said bluntly, "The muckrakers were never willing to admit that collectivism was the
only permanent check upon the enslavement of the people
by the most amazing plutocracy in the world."[7]

5. ATTACK ON THE BOSSES

A new school of political reformers took up where the
Mugwumps left off. It is often difficult to find the line of

demarcation, for they both used much the same rhetoric. Mugwumpery is essentially a negative conception. It conceives of the politician in terms of what he should not do rather than in terms of what he should do. He should not harbor prostitutes, he should not steal public funds, he should not grant too generous franchises. In short, he should not betray the public interest. He has all these restraints, yet he has little positive responsibility. Moreover the Mugwumps were often backed by conservative groups who felt that the plundering of city treasuries was bad for business and that the services which they expected from government were badly administered.

On the other hand, these new reformers were aware that potent interests had entrenched themselves in the government for malevolent purposes. In the 1870's the agrarian movement led to the setting up of commissions to regulate the railroads. And in 1890 the Sherman Act had been passed as a resolution against the formation of monopolies. But the commissions were not successful nor was the anti-trust resolution any better. Why? Because the whole legal and political framework through which the measures must be made effective were in enemy hands. The courts were obstructive, the administrators unreliable; and when public sentiment had died down it was easy for the interests to buy back the legislature and wipe off the regulation. Now they hoped to recover the government for themselves. It must become their instrument, and they would expect their representatives to supply municipal traction, state-wide regulation of insurance, railroads and banks and national regulation of food and natural resources. They were attacking the bosses because they were the enemy in the first-line trenches.

In the beginning these reformers were most conspicuous in the cities. The Rev. Dr. Parkhurst, for example, arose in New York to overthrow Tammany Hall and its business connections. But it was not so simple as that. The city machine was but a part of the state system. So Joseph Folk, circuit attorney of St. Louis in 1899, found that he would have to become Governor of Missouri (as he did in 1904) if he were really to free St. Louis from the domination of the utilities. And Governor Robert La Follette felt that he could not complete his work until he went on to the United States Senate.

At the turn of the century there was a virtual renaissance of political liberators—Tom L. Johnson in Cleveland, Samuel M. Jones in Toledo, and Jacob Coxey in Massilon, Ohio. And there was a curious carry-over of the Mugwump ideal. These men, for the most part, were not merely progressive politicians carrying out a program. They regarded themselves as the harbingers of a new moral era. In their midst were clergymen and millionaires endowed with a conscience by Henry George's books. Now they proceeded from moral leadership to institutional reform. They had, of course, inherited civil service reform and the Australian ballot from their forerunners, the Mugwumps. Votes could no longer be bought outright, but the bosses could still manipulate candidates at the conventions.

The elder La Follette, for one, set about to make the party itself more accessible to the people. He started a movement for the direct primary system and established it in Wisconsin in 1903. The movement spread so rapidly that by 1910 two-thirds of the states had adopted the Wisconsin Idea. Oregon was the inspiration for another series of innovations, beginning with the direct legislation machinery, the initiative and referendum in 1903, which was widely emulated in the other states, and proceeding in 1908 with an act for the recall of judges, which was more controversial and less widely emulated. At the end of the decade White evaluated these reforms thus:

"Capital is not eliminated from politics, but it is not the dominant force it was ten years ago. . . . Each of these innovations, the secret ballot, the primary, and the reformed party is a step towards democracy—a step towards the Declaration of Independence and away from the Constitution, which so feared majority rule that the majority was hedged about with checks and balances at every possible point."[8]

The same progressive impulse led, on the federal level, to the Seventeenth Amendment, which provided for the popular election of Senators. As might be anticipated, the bosses in the Senate put up stubborn resistance, for the Senate, whose members were elected by state legislatures, was one of the most secluded and undemocratic bodies in our system. The House had passed resolutions for direct election of Senators in 1894, 1898, 1900, and 1902. But the Senate under the leadership of such intransigents as George F. Hoar of Massachusetts refused to commit what they regarded as institutional suicide, until finally two Insurgent Republicans, William E. Borah and Joseph Bristow of Kansas, saw it through in 1911. Two years later the Amendment was ratified.

6. TRUST-BUSTING

The politician was being reformed. The people were once more in command of the visible government. But it was not enough. The invisible government with all its vast economic powers was still firmly entrenched. Progressives now took their second logical step in attacking the great evil. They shifted their emphasis from the political to the economic field.

Historically you can watch this sequence in one state after another—as, for example, in California under Hiram Johnson and in New York under Charles Evans Hughes. The reformers first routed out the party bosses through the innovation of direct primaries. Then they proceeded to pass corporation taxes, utility and insurance regulations.

With this phase, the progressives began to operate through their own political organizations and leaders. Now that they were in the seats of power, they developed a degree of cynicism about political practice. As the reformer becomes preoccupied with more fundamental aspects of the evil, he becomes increasingly tolerant of the surface aspects. He is less prone to blame the boss than to blame the interest behind the boss. And in fact, if the boss will listen to the promptings of the new regime, the reformer will not hesitate to compromise with him.

The case of Theodore Roosevelt is instructive. He began life as a civil service reformer, but as he rose to the top he grew less and less scrupulous. To be sure, during his Presidential terms he extended the civil service classifications, but he found that economic reform was a much more burning issue. And for that purpose he worked with and through the regular Republican bosses, Aldrich in the Senate and Joe Cannon in the House. Feeling the deflationary compulsions of his program, he developed an intense dislike for the Mugwump spirit and for the muckrakers whom he branded forever with that name. In an essay, *Latitude and Longitude among Reformers*, he wrote characteristically:

> "They [the Mugwump reformers] do not do practical work, and the extreme folly of their position makes them not infrequently the allies of scoundrels who cynically practise corruption. Too often, indeed, they actually alienate from the cause of decency keen and honest men, who grow to regard all movements for reform with contemptuous dislike because of the folly and vanity of the men who in the name of righteousness preach unwisdom and practise uncharitableness."[9]

In the work of progressivism, he explained, the desire to do good is not enough. It must be combined with efficiency, the ability to achieve that ideal in the practical world.   And he blandly proceeded to discuss the nature and uses of compromise.

> "It is not possible to lay down an inflexible rule as to when compromise is right and when wrong; when it is a sign of the highest statesmanship to temporize, and when it is merely a proof of weakness.   Now and then one can stand uncompromisingly for a naked principle and force people up to it.   This is always the attractive course; but in certain great crises it may be a very wrong course.   Compromise, in the proper sense, merely means agreement; in the proper sense, opportunism should merely mean doing the best possible with actual conditions as they exist."[10]

This attitude did not sit very well with a number of the reformers of the day.   Ray Stannard Baker, for example, retorted:

> "In the beginning, I thought and still think, he [Theodore Roosevelt] did great good in giving support to the movement. But I did not believe then, and have never believed since, that these ills can be settled by partisan political methods.   They are moral and economic questions.   A movement ought to have been built up slowly and solidly from the bottom."[11]

The chief concern of this economic phase was to restrain the trusts from exacting a greater toll than they deserved. In this endeavor many reforms of an enduring nature were devised.   Income taxes and corporation taxes were adopted in many states to restore some of the plunder to the people. In the states there was a great increase of all kinds of commissions for the control of railroads, utilities, banks and insurance companies.   On the federal plane there was the Railroad Rate Act of 1906, the Food Inspection Act, and land conservation.

Here were a variety of ways of varying effectiveness to moderate the ravages of corporate power.   But through all this increasing sophistication the old moral indignation still flourished.   It seemed a more direct way of piercing the thick hides of the economic dinosaurs. Invoke the Sherman Act. Theodore Roosevelt exploited these emotional appeals to the full. It made little difference whether trusts were good or bad. Although he knew that nothing very tangible could be gained, he engaged in shadow-boxing, prosecuting the Northern Securities Company in 1904 and Standard Oil and the Tobacco Trust in 1907. There were formal dissolutions in each case, but the economic power remained intact.

He did succeed, however, in giving the voters a thrill of righteous satisfaction. At last they had seen the wicked trusts chastised by the federal government. It was a splendid concession to their idealism. Unscrupulous individuals were at fault for the present state of society. So the President arrested the most conspicuous offenders, put them in the stocks for a few months, whipped them— and then let them go, with their institutions unchanged. What more could he have done? He might have strung them up by the neck; but that would have carried idealism to a point of impracticability. To the progressive mind of the day he was on the right track; he arrested the right people. For monopolies were then conceived of as a group of men committing a moral offense; it was appropriate that the punishment likewise be moral.

From this point of view trust-busting was eminently successful. The heads of the corporations, described and treated as criminals, went about their business in a much more modest and God-fearing way. They sought popular reprieve by good behaviour. They developed a palpable conscience, exhibited through expressions of concern for employees, stockholders, and consumers, and through the employment of public relations counsel. Norman Hapgood, surveying the results of trust-busting at the end of the era, wrote:

"When I was a boy, the hostility to the first faint protests of the less fortunate was confident and decisive. Mark Hanna's era marked the climax of this easy defiance by the strong. I well remember the charming, bulldog manner with which Hanna took up the defense of unlimited private monopoly, in reply to Mr. Bryan's attacks on the trusts. It was a note that can never be sounded quite so fearlessly again. Even Mr. Gary has to watch a little, to catch the favorable moment, in order to get all of the great organs of established privilege on his side. Even he cannot be as gay as Hanna was.

"Surely history will be just to Col. Roosevelt. It will call him the first American of enormous popularity and ability to question the modern industrial system."[12]

CHAPTER FOUR

Progressive Ambitions: 1912–1940

1. Wilson's New Freedom
2. The New Deal
3. Obsolescence

1. WILSON'S NEW FREEDOM

AT THIS point in the history of American progressivism we cross the Great Divide. The progressives outgrew their efforts to reform wicked individuals, bosses and robber barons, and acquired a much broader vision. They no longer regarded evil as confined to any one group in society. The whole pattern of interrelated parts was considered at fault. They discovered that we were living under a "system" and that there existed other and better systems for which we must strive. Their moral conception of society, wherein the standards of goodness applied only to individuals, developed into a systemic conception with standards by which society as a whole could be judged.

And when the evil was discovered to be not only widespread in existing society, but also rooted in the past, there was even greater assurance of its systemic character. Charles Beard, for example, in the *Economic Interpretation of the Constitution* (1908) simply went a step further than the muckrakers. He accepted their thesis that economic interests controlled the visible government and proceeded to trace this control back into our historic beginnings. He found that even the Founding Fathers, consciously or unconsciously, were heirs to the same pressures. Our Constitution itself was molded according to economic demands. With this discovery the moral wrath of the muckrakers subsided. They could hardly condemn wealthy interests that had been wicked since the very beginning.

About this time—1907 to 1914—a number of writers appeared with plans for a systematic overhauling of American society: Herbert Croly with *The Promise of American Life* (1908), J. Allen Smith, with *The Spirit of American Government* (1907), Walter Weyl with *The New Democracy* (1912), Walter Lippmann with his *Preface to Politics* (1913) and others. It was, in a sense, the emergence of an intellectual wing of the progressive movement, symbolized in 1914 by the founding of *The New Republic*. The dispassionate intellectual began to flourish in the era of social engineering, where clergymen had flourished in the era of uplift.

The Presidential campaign of 1912 introduced these schemes into the political forum for the first time. For his part Theodore Roosevelt, whose facile tongue had preached almost every type of reform from Mugwump civil service to trust-busting, now encompassed the New Nationalism. He concocted this along the lines of Croly's notion of a Hamiltonian state dispensing industrial justice, and revised his trust policy to a point where he would license large enterprises. He had finally lifted the moral onus from individual trusts and placed it on the system.

On his side Woodrow Wilson saw the issue as a struggle between oligarchy and democracy—the two rival systems. In the New Nationalism, he saw nothing but a variation on the oligarchic theme. There was still an uneasy partnership between government and the licensed interests, for the

interests would undoubtedly have the final word. Thus
he berated Roosevelt:

> "The thought of the people of the United States has not yet
> penetrated to your consciousness. You are willing to act *for*
> the people, but you are not willing to act *through* the people."[1]

Wilson advocated a system, the New Freedom, in which
the energies of the people might find full expression. Government, he said, must keep open the channels by which
common men rise to prominence, for the common man is
the source of our greatness. He is the eternal replenisher
of the genius of American life. Looking about him Wilson
found the channels clogged. The party bosses stifled the
political expression of the common man, and the monopolists stifled his business expression.

In office he proceeded to give material form to the New
Freedom as well as he could. He sponsored the Federal
Reserve Act in 1913, by which credit facilities might be
extended to the small business man, and he ensured lower
interest rates for farm loans. He secured a downward
revision of the tariff in the Underwood Act of the same year,
thus removing some of the special privileges of big interests.
He sponsored the Clayton Anti-Trust Act of 1914, which
penalized unfair trade practices and attempted to enforce
competition. Finally, he sought to protect labor by such
legislation as a clause in the Clayton Act exempting trade
unions from the anti-trust legislation, the Child Labor Act,
later invalidated by the Supreme Court, and the Adamson
Act which provided for an eight-hour day for railroad employees.

It was almost inevitable in this evolution of attitudes
that when the progressives found a new level of expression,
they withdrew their energies from the old level. Theodore
Roosevelt, emerging into his trust-busting phase, became

quite indifferent to the political evils which he had earlier scourged. So Woodrow Wilson on entering the systemic phase was fairly indifferent to both preceding phases. He did not seem at all concerned about the evils of the party organization. He did not share Senator Norris's favorite indignation. In fact, he exploited that organization to the full, very much on the English pattern. In a letter to Senator Thornton of Louisiana, he wrote:

> "No party can ever for any length of time control the Government or serve the people which can not command the allegiance of its own minority. I feel that there are times, when those who are overruled should accept the principle of party government and act with the colleagues through whom they expect to see the country best served."[2]

Thus Wilson was no prude. If the parties had been organized autocratically in the past in the interests of plunder, he would organize his party just as autocratically in the interests of a progressive program. And he would employ every means at his disposal to bring wayward Congressmen into line. David Lawrence reports:

> "Mr. Wilson's impulse as President-elect was to carry his program of reform to the uttermost. He would have liked to see the seniority rule abandoned in the selection of committee chairmen in Congress so that progressives, or men in close sympathy with his ideas, might lead in the preparation of legislation. But the practical difficulties in the way of such reform impressed [him]. . . . Rather did Mr. Wilson decide that he could accomplish the same result by converting men who had been reactionaries into progressives so far as their votes were concerned."[3]

Nor did Wilson become so highly aroused about the trusts as did the first Roosevelt. He opposed monopolies. He did not attempt to justify them as either inevitable or economically efficient. But he was very calm in his opposition.

Monopolies, he said in his New Freedom speeches, were artificial stop-gaps in an essentially mobile economy. The monopolists were not wicked. They had ventured upon a policy of stifling competition and of acting as the trustees for the people simply as the easiest road to success. He did not blame them. It was not their fault. It was the fault of the system which allowed such a course.

There we see the curious spectacle of the progressive expanding his engineering projects in one direction and his cynicism in another. If Wilson had a wider scope for his ideals than Norris or Theodore Roosevelt he also had a wider scope for his indifference. Progressivism changed its character. It grew from a moral pursuit of witches to the more cold-blooded business of drawing blueprints for large-scale, but mild, social reconstructions.

2. THE NEW DEAL

During the 1920's the progressives developed little further in the scope of their ambitions. Conservatism was on the offensive and while Congress was at a standstill, the courts were slowly undoing the work of a previous era. The elder La Follette in his Progressive campaign for President in 1924 reiterated the old bromides: higher inheritance taxes, government ownership of railroads, abolition of child labor, direct election of the President, a federal initiative and referendum, and the power of Congress to override judicial veto. The farm bloc in Congress pressed for subsidies without success. Perhaps the most pertinent issue of that day was not the forward movement of democratization, but the maintenance of civil liberties against the anti-radical and Ku Klux Klan hysteria.

In 1933 the New Deal brought on a progressive renaissance. It brought with it the scope of the New Freedom. It was, for example, equally cynical in its use and exploitation of the political party. Moreover, for the first time a progressive administration could beat the conservatives at their own game, for they long had at their disposal Jim Farley, one of the most skilful and successful political organizers since the heyday of Mark Hanna. And when Senator Hatch sought to curtail some of the political excesses of the New Deal, particularly the use of the WPA in the elections of 1938, the New Dealers in Congress proceeded to fight his first bill openly and his second bill covertly.

Yet many progressives still refuse to reconcile the unsavory aspects of party machinery with the cause of reform, although every such administration since Cleveland has necessarily employed them. We find this outmoded protest of John T. Flynn in *The New Republic* in reference to the Horner scandals in Illinois:

> "As long as I can remember, the progressive, liberal, and radical groups in America have been waging war upon these slush funds. All the statutes against corrupt practises have originated with them. It was not until the last seven years and in the present administration that these two-per cent funds have been gilded over with the respectability which now seems to cover all sorts of things which were once regarded as corrupt—campaign books sold in bulk to corporations, two-per cent squeezes upon officeholders, Jackson Day dinners (another scheme for squeezing officeholders), together with numerous other devices to swell private profit, such as capitalizing high office and position to make money on radio contracts and other forms of gain. Cannot the great liberal groups leave these devices to their enemies?"[4]

Nor were the New Dealers particularly shocked by the existence of holding companies in the economy. They turned corporate witch-hunting into a fairly refined and sophisticated device, to be employed in the achievement of a larger program, when they found it necessary to tighten up tax laws, secure new regulations, or, as in the winter of 1938, to break the "strike of capital".

But the New Dealers added something new to the growing progressive tradition. They could no longer proceed to change the oligarchic system into a democracy in the old leisurely way. The job was now forced on them by its spontaneous collapse in the Great Depression. Whether they wanted to or not, they had to take over the functions of business investment; and reform, for the first time, became largely synonymous with recovery. Truly, progressivism had come a long way from spiritual uplift.

Progressivism threw in its lot against the business cycle. President Roosevelt expressed this very clearly. In the introduction to his public papers, he said, "A catastrophe seems to have been necessary to focus attention once more on ideals in government." Then he set out the goal of recovery for all economic groups and added, "We were . . . determined to effect reform where abuses existed in order to make our recovery a more lasting one."[5] And in one of his speeches, he said, "We have always known that heedless self-interest was bad morals; we now know that it is bad economics."

The consequences of this change have been far reaching. First of all, the New Dealers have found a way of restating the progressive ideal more concretely. For Wilson democracy was a qualitative norm; it was a state of society in which there would be the maximum expression for the maximum number of people. It would be achieved, in Plato's words, when there would be rendered "unto each his due." This conception had the great disadvantage that you could never tell exactly where you were on the road to democracy. The ideal of a mobile economy was abstract. At any point in his years of reform Wilson might have announced that the ideal had been attained, and many people would have believed him. The only proof to the contrary was the continued existence of the immobile structures in the economy—the holding companies. And the only proof that he was even moving in the right direction lay in the fact that these vested interests opposed his reforms.

Franklin Roosevelt also maintains this ideal. He still talks of "social justice," "economic democracy" and the "more abundant life." But he has succeeded in translating the qualitative norm into a statistical norm, from vague phrases about justice to exact statements as to the national income and how it is distributed. This does not reflect any greater ingenuity on his part, but rather the compulsions of the times. For the oligarchy running its unchastened course in the 1920's had brought on a social wreckage that could be neatly inventoried. There were so many millions unemployed. There was so much idle plant capacity. There was such a decrease in the national income. If unregulated oligarchy did all that, said F. D. R., we must make reforms, and the test of these reforms will lie in the degree to which we eliminate depressions. In other words, when we have converted our oligarchy into an economic democracy our success will be recorded in the business indices.

The second consequence of this ideal of social engineering has been its extreme flexibility. It may be used to justify a vast range of policies. For with our limited knowledge of economic consequences, the administration can argue for almost any measure on the grounds that it will increase the national income. Thus, the New Deal encompasses in its wide bosom such various functions as government as regulator of capitalist excesses (SEC, TVA), government as underwriter of capitalist failings (RFC, HOLC, AAA, NRA), government as champion of the small business man (Holding Company Act, prosecutions under the Sherman Act), government as patron of the trade unions (Wagner Act, Wage and Hour Act), government as dispenser of social services (Social Security, housing and slum clearance).

This flexibility may lead to great internal contradictions, but they are all made plausible by that all-encompassing rationalization—namely, the restoration of the national income. The New Deal approach to trusts is a case in point. Under the NRA it tolerated and even encouraged monopolistic practises in certain industries and even now it shows evidence of paternalism, as in its treatment of the bituminous coal industry. More recently, under the Robert Jackson-Thurman Arnold regime, it has prosecuted unfair practises among milk distributors, oil distributors, and motion picture distributors. Yet the New Dealers betray no embarrassment. Every industry, they say, must be analyzed in terms of the role it plays in the production of national wealth. Competition in one industry may be harmful to the economy, while in another industry it should be encouraged. If there has been an appearance of confusion and indecision, they argue, it is because the problem is so vast and the solution necessarily so complex.

Thirdly, there has been a new impetus to progressivism. It is the great virtue of "pump priming" that it is at the same time a palliative for the revival of investment and a boon to the impoverished "one-third of a nation." Hence, it secures the support of eminent economists and certain enlightened business men as well as of progressives. And those economists who see no other way out are often led by a Keynesian logic to a position even more radical than that of the New Deal. With the uncertainties of an economy, half private investment and half public investment, half free and half planned, they pose the question whether or not the government should not go the whole hog. It is conceivable that the new demands of the business cycle may supply a dynamic drive that will move us far faster than our normal stride.

Franklin Roosevelt has done a host of things for which Theodore Roosevelt and Woodrow Wilson would have been denounced as rank socialists. And he has, more or less, got away with it. He has spent billions of dollars on work relief on the grounds that he was priming the pump for private enterprise. He has fostered wage and hour acts and fathered the trade unions—all on the grounds that the workers must get a larger share of purchasing power. He has ventured into the field of cheap power production in the TVA—not in order to compete with private utilities, he says, but to bring about the economic rejuvenation of the Tennessee Valley area and to control floods.

And what is the price of this deflation? Progressivism, restated in terms of its role in the business cycle, has lost much of its poetry and moral content. Imagine an ideal place like Heaven being described as an economy with 40% of the milk in the hands of 70% of its immortal population and 70% of the honey in the hands of 40% of the population. Yet that is precisely the deflation that the New Deal has wrought upon the progressive ideal. Such disenchantment could only flourish in these post-war and Fascist years. When capitalism was in its ascendency, the progressives could afford the luxury of a Platonic dream. Now with capitalism *in extremis*, all they can ask is that the system keep working and providing a minimum of life's necessities. We have reduced a rich heritage of hopes and dreams to the bare endeavor to make the system work.

Now I, for one, am willing to pay this price. I believe that in the past we progressives have not been sufficiently matter-of-fact. Moral and spiritual objectives have obscured material objectives; and it has taken a succession of crises to bring us down to earth and to confine our natural exuberance within useful bounds.   Yet there is something to be said on the other side.   Perhaps our programs have been so shaped by the crises of the moment that in a future without crises, domestic or foreign, we should be at a loss as to what to do.

The New Deal is so wide in its scope, so tolerant of the most dubious experiments that it lacks any sense of direction or continuity.   The developmental implications of the various measures fly off at tangents—often in contradiction to one another.   Its ideal of economic democracy has been negative.   With capitalism *in extremis*, the progressives had only to restore the economy to its capacity production of 1929 introducing only such reforms in the distribution of purchasing power as were necessary to ensure a greater stability.   Like drowning men we have been happy to get back on the same raft, though slightly repaired, from which we toppled.   We know where we came from (that is, the bottom of the depression), but, once returned, we are not sure where we are going, whether towards Fascism or socialism or somewhere else.   As an attempt to emerge from this crisis, helter-skelter groping for economic straws may be all very well.   But if we are to effect positive social reconstruction we shall need more than that.   We shall have to point the way towards greater productivity than ever before.   And we must adopt a more explicit plan.

3. OBSOLESCENCE

Now if the progressives really changed their scope and ambitions at such frequent and marked intervals as I have indicated, one may well ask about the fate of the progressive who survived from one period of progressivism into another.   It is by no means an academic question.   We have many cases of such survivals.   A few were able to adjust themselves to the changing conditions. Others, less flexible, lost touch with their time and cluttered up the progressive army with their vestigial reputations.

Indeed, it was not to be wondered at that some old progressives opposed F. D. R.'s Court Plan. To any one who has read our recent history, such development was part of an inevitable process. The average progressive has an alarming rate of obsolescence. After about ten years of service he is washed up. His valves are stuck, his cogs blunted and his pipes rusted. And when those elder statesmen fell out with the President it was no more than could be expected.

If we were less sentimental about our public men we would retire them as soon as they showed signs of decay. But they refuse to retire at the end of one historical era. They insist on surviving into the next. They demand audience on grounds of their past eminence and cry down the men who have succeeded them. Hence we have to contend not only with the living, but also with the living dead. I believe politics would be much simpler if we were rid of such zombies as Al Smith, Hiram Johnson, Carter Glass and Burton Wheeler.

But we learned something about humanity as well as efficiency during the nineteenth century. And the survival of the fittest which prevailed in the jungle no longer prevails at the polls of the world's richest nation. We are kind to those who have outlived their fitness and we venerate antiques of all kinds. Perhaps it is more than kindness. Perhaps these men are deliberately kept alive, not by their old friends but by their old enemies, who know that they can be of great service to conservatism in their decline. Perhaps their obsolescence as progressives only means their rebirth on the other side. At any rate, it is a sorry spectacle, and one can only question the nature of a conservatism that draws its mightiest champions from derelict and tired liberals.

There have been many explanations of this obsolescence. Some argue that the life of the progressive is so hard, so solitary and subject to such criticism that few can stand it more than ten years, especially as old age approaches. Others emphasize the temptations of going over to the other side, the promise of fame, publicity, riches and easy acceptance. Still others talk of resentment at the rise of new and more dynamic leaders, or the sense of having completed a program.

I favor a different explanation. I have already described the growth of progressive ambitions, how progressives have undertaken larger and larger engineering projects approaching collectivism and, at the same time, have decreased their concern for the moralities. Though history may take this course it is an exceedingly difficult course for the individual. For it means efficiency at the cost of moral indignation. It means steadily decreasing spiritual returns, a retrogression from a belief in high angelic standards to a concern for filling the animal needs of the community. We do not like to become deflated. We find it much easier to move upwards from cynicism to high moral attitudes than to move downward in the opposite direction.

Oswald Garrison Villard began his political life under the tutelage of the Mugwumps, of Godkin and Schurz. He has fought the good fight so well that now he has acquired the reputation of being the "Dean of American Liberals." Yet, strangely enough, he has never fully accepted the ideals of any leader since his nonage, T. R.'s trust-busting, or Wilson's New Freedom; and he has been continually carping at the debaucheries of the New Deal. And no wonder, for he never really escaped the spiritual hold of his

Mugwump tutors. He has vacillated between the desire for Good Government and the equally impossible Socialism of Norman Thomas. The only President who ever captured his heart, he confessed, was Grover Cleveland. Why? Because Cleveland had the integrity to go down to certain defeat in the election of 1888 rather than compromise on the tariff issue. In short Villard was obsolescent even before he started. He explains:

> "To my mind the high-water mark of personal virtue and patriotic service in the White House in my life time was that scene when, in 1888, Mr. Cleveland called in his chief political advisers and lieutenants to talk to them about the coming presidential campaign. He did not ask them what he should do so far as his own fortunes were concerned; he did not ask them what political issues he should espouse. When they had assembled, he told them he had determined to stand for re-election and on the issue of tariff for revenue only. Promptly every man in the room protested.... "Well then, gentlemen," said Grover Cleveland, "*I shall* be defeated."—and he was. It is strange that it is necessary to portray this simple, and normal, and conscientious stand as the greatest act of moral courage by a President in fifty years—but that it is. Not one of his successors would, in my judgment, have been capable of a similar greatness."[6]

Indeed this resistence to deflation has characterized almost every new progressive upsurge. And the old generation has almost always deplored the new generation as immoral and debauched. Of course they are right. For morality is obviously on their side, and mere efficiency on that of their successors. Look at the reaction of the Mugwumps who lived past their prime into the period of the Populists and the trust-busters. Grover Cleveland, Carl Schurz and E. L. Godkin experienced the pangs of obsolescence and righteously retired into the camp of the enemy.

The Democratic Convention of 1896 witnessed the first expulsion of the angels. There Cleveland, after years of struggle in Congress, lost control of his party to the agrarian silver agitators. Cleveland indicted the whole new order, yet he had no misgivings about himself or about the people's ultimate return to Mugwumpery. In a letter to Don M. Dickenson, dated Feb. 18, 1896, he wrote,

> "You know my supreme faith in the American people. While I believe them to be just now deluded, mistaken, and wickedly duped, they will certainly return to sound principles and patriotic aspirations; and what I may suffer in the period of aberration is not important. . . . I cannot be mistaken in believing that if the Democratic party is to survive, its banner upon which shall be inscribed its true principles and safe policies, must be held aloft by sturdy hands which even though few, will in the gloom of defeat, save it from the disgraceful clutch of time-serving camp followers and knavish traitors."[7]

Thus Cleveland went into exile, helping the Republicans, high-tariff and all, rather than support a deflated doctrine. He tried to secure control of the party in 1900 but failed. In 1904 he rejoiced in the candidacy of the conservative Alton Parker, despite the apathy of the country. Trust-busting was the order of the day and Teddy Roosevelt was its greatest exponent. As progressivism evolved in ever more ambitious scope Cleveland became a bitter old man. Towards his death he wrote in a letter to Commodore Benedict,

> "I see our President [T. R.] has been making another 'Yes I guess not' speech on business, corporations, etc. and has told the farmers how completely they should have the land and the fullness thereof; Gov. Hughes seems to be attempting neck-breaking acrobatics; Bryan smiles at both of them while performing his continuous tight-rope dance; and Hearst in his cage of wild beasts waits his turn to surprise and shock the multitude—'Open every hour of the day and night, gentlemen: wonderful vaudeville performance—all seen under one tent.' "[8]

Meanwhile Carl Schurz, the leader of the Independent Republican movement against Grant in 1872 and of the Cleveland cause in 1884, found life equally unpleasant. Confronted with the spectacle of Bryanism and free silver, he turned about and supported McKinley. Hardly had McKinley's administration got under way when the Spanish war broke out. This was too much. For if Mugwumpery was anything it was anti-imperialist, and it was certainly ironic that after its greatest travail in the Democratic Party, it should now find equal travail with its new friends in the Republican Party. Mugwumpery had been evicted from both parties, and fled to the wilderness.

Moreover when Theodore Roosevelt became President there was an even more tragic spectacle. For the Mugwumps had once claimed him as their own. He had been an exemplary Civil Service Commissioner under Harrison, but now became contemptuous of his former associates. He reviled them for not sharing his enthusiasm for empire. He called them weaklings and pacifists. And Schurz spent his last days pleading with his wayward friend.

Perhaps the bitterest of all Mugwumps was E. L. Godkin. For he was, after all, the theorist of the Mugwump movement. He carried his opposition to its logical fullness, and revealed himself, consistent to be sure, but conservative, even reactionary, to an absurd degree. He shared with the other Mugwumps the bitterness over free silver and the imperialism of 1898. But he went further. He opposed the railroad legislation in the states, defended the carriers against charges of watered stock to the point of ignoring the obvious, and defended the courts from the attack made upon them in the Democratic platform of 1896.

> "Judicial decisions have again and again drawn the fangs of confiscatory and revolutionary legislation, and the courts have come more and more to stand as the great bulwarks of property and personal rights."[9]

Nonetheless the spiritual appeal of "good men" has persisted as an ingredient of every reform movement, tempering the harsh process of institutional change. Mayor LaGuardia of New York adopts the New Deal spirit in his city administration. He has prided himself on his relief system, his services to the community, the parks and the city-owned subways, his tolerance of union organization and of the most seditious agitations. He has been supported by the American Labor Party, which has potentialities far more radical than the Democratic New Deal. And yet he could never have been elected Mayor if he had not had in his program an ancient brand of Mugwumpery, on which he flaunted his high moral stature in contrast to the knavery of Tammany Hall. And on this ground he received the support of the Republicans, side by side with that of the Laborites, making a clean sweep of the political spectrum.

But for the most part Mugwumpery has been the last stand of scoundrels. When a party can think of no institutional changes with which to meet our problems it resorts to the moralities. Thus for a while, the Republicans, unable to find a constructive alternative to the New Deal, took to their hearts the District Attorney of New York, Tom Dewey. Mr. Dewey did not pretend to know the institutional cure for unemployment or for the raising of the national income. But he did know the cure for dishonesty. He had made a brilliant record in cleaning up the local rackets and their political connections within the Democratic Party. He had shown himself to be not only righteous, but dramatically righteous, in combating the unrighteous. Many people felt that his righteousness would be equally telling when confronted with the unholy mess of the American economy.

All of which was obviously atavistic, a measure of Republican despair. The surprising thing was that he acquired such a following that the New Deal was forced to include some Mugwumpery among its other palliatives; and the Attorney-General did some house-cleaning within the Democracies of Missouri and Louisiana.

In somewhat less striking degree, the agrarians and Populists, in turn, became obsolete with the triumph of Wilson's New Freedom. Here were differing degrees of sophistication, and many observers were struck by the anachronism of William Jennings Bryan, the silver voice of the West in 1896, sitting in the Cabinet as Secretary of State under the urbane Woodrow Wilson. For when Wilson pressed the bill setting up the Federal Reserve system, it was, in a sense, a systemic approach to the very problem which had given rise to the free silver agitation—namely, the need for a flexible credit system. Many of the old Bryanites in Congress were suspicious of the bill, fearing that it was an instrument of Wall Street. But Wilson convinced the Commoner as you might convince a harness-maker of the greater efficiency of automobiles. With a kind of pathetic acceptance Bryan passed on the word to his followers and the bill was passed.

The stormy petrel, Tom Watson, also survived, maintaining control of Georgia off and on until his death in 1924. There he preached the most diverse and unpredictable doctrines. When the Populist ferment subsided in the South he passed to the other extreme, conducting crusades against Negroes, Catholics and Jews; and he has been credited with the revival of the Ku Klux Klan. Yet he also cultivated the anti-imperialist bias that he had caught during the Spanish-American War, and when we became involved in the First World War he criticized the whole business from Woodrow Wilson and the suppression of civil liberties under A. Mitchell Palmer down to the formation of the American Legion.

It was fortunate that most of the other Populist leaders

died at the closing of their era. For though they died in
defeat, they were at least spared the pangs of obsolescence.
Ignatius Donnelly, who ran as the Populist nominee for
Vice-President in 1900, died a few months later, a drift
towards spiritualism developing at the end. Henry Demarest Lloyd, who had written the original muckraking volume,
Wealth Against Commonwealth, turned to the Socialists and
joined their party shortly before his death in 1903. "Sockless" Jerry Simpson, who had carried the standard in
Congress, was retired to private life in 1898, and after some
adventures in journalism died four years later.

If the Grim Reaper spared many Populists the embarrassment of surviving into the Progressive Era it did little
to mollify the lot of those who have survived from the
Progressive Era into the heyday of the New Deal. Indeed
these men have, for the most part, so established their reputations in the ranks of conservatism that we have forgotten
the scenes of their youth and of their liberal glory. Who
remembers today that William Randolph Hearst was a
muckraker and trust-buster of such violence that he was
called the Robespierre of American progressivism? Who
remembers that Chief Justice Charles Evans Hughes and
Senator Hiram Johnson were two of the great reform
Governors? Who remembers that Justice McReynolds was
a leading prosecutor of the trusts, both under T. R. and
Woodrow Wilson? Or that Burton K. Wheeler, during the
World War decade, was the bitterest antagonist of the
copper interests in Montana? Or that Carter Glass was
one of the leading lights of the New Freedom? Such, indeed, are the ravages of time.

These men have not necessarily moved backwards.
Other leaders have simply moved forward, and they have
failed to follow. They stay behind, clinging to their repu-

tations and defining as progressive their stand of some twenty-odd years ago. They overlook the fact that progressivism, by its very nature, cannot be defined at any one point by abstract and immutable principles. Thus, for example, the *New York Herald Tribune* protests against F. D. R.'s claim that the New Deal alone has charted the progressive front of the 1930's. They write ironically:

"Senator Hiram Johnson, of California, in his surprised innocence, resents the President's charge that he is no longer liberal. He thinks it is President Roosevelt who has changed. He should have known that the moment he ceased supporting the New Deal he ceased being liberal even though eight years ago, Mr. Roosevelt hailed him as the greatest liberal of our time."[10]

Yet what they write in irony, I believe to be literally true· It is the generals who define a battlefield, not wayward and tired lieutenants; and that battlefield is much more likely to be where the enemy is thickest today than where he was routed a generation ago.

It is heartening, indeed, that a chosen few, like Senator Norris, can survive in a changing scope and declining morality and still stick to the cause. Norris made his reputation by his attack on the bosses, and by the toppling of "Uncle Joe" Cannon, the Speaker of the House, from his all powerful position. Yet he has been able to maintain a lonely but consistent leadership throughout the years, fighting for public power, and finding in the New Deal, and particularly in the achievement of the TVA, a fulfilment rather than a perversion of his progressive dreams. To be sure throughout that time he has retained the bugaboos of the Progressive Era. He still argues for the direct election of the President. He continues to find party organization a betrayal of the people, and has had a notorious distaste for Jim Farley and the organizational aspects of the New Deal.   But he has not permitted his outmoded prejudices to interfere with his faith in the moving front of the progressive struggle.

In this category I place also Louis Brandeis who, although associated with the economics of the New Freedom, continues to stand as inspiration for the inner circle of New Dealers and Felix Frankfurter who has contributed much to the New Deal personnel as well as to its strategy.   By their gift for legal innovation, these men have themselves symbolized the shift from moral to engineering reform since the time of Woodrow Wilson.   And the young Senator La Follette, who might have been hampered by the slightly obsolete heritage of his father and who today shares that Middle Western disability in the field of foreign policy, continues to plod on with the same pains and courage, a champion of civil liberties and a friend of President Roosevelt.

CHAPTER FIVE

Withdrawal of the Puritan

1. Separation of Church and State
2. The Puritan Wing
3. Puritans in Decline
4. Will They Come Back?

I. SEPARATION OF CHURCH AND STATE

THE Puritans have been less in evidence during the New Deal than during any comparable reform period in our recent history. And that is for the best. Progressives have been free to concentrate on legitimate political and economic aims. They have been free to do something about the security of the submerged "one-third of the nation", letting the moral by-products of their insecurity—prostitution, alcoholism and gambling—either take care of themselves or be taken in hand by the clergy and social welfare agencies.

The association of Puritanism with progressive politics is very old, older than the American Revolution. The Great Rebellion of Cromwell, it will be recalled, was as much a religious and moral revolt of the Puritans as it was a political revolt against the tyranny of Charles I. And the rebels celebrated their victory by closing up the theatres as dens of unrighteousness and by clothing all Britain in gray and sombre clothes. To a lesser extent the French Revolution was also a Puritan revolt. It produced a vice crusade which raged in the midst of the Terror and sent

many prostitutes to the guillotine. There were two in-
dictments: first, that prostitution was contrary to natural
restraints as set out in the doctrines of Jean Jaques Rousseau, and second, that these ladies held strong Royalist
sympathies because they had been parasites of the aristocracy.

There can be little wonder, therefore, that Puritans were
inextricably bound up with American expressions of political
protest, both in the American Revolution itself, and more
so in the great reform movements of the nineteenth century,
when morality pervaded almost all our political activity.
The Puritan program was the natural concomitant of an
inflated ideal. The Mugwumps supervised the behavior
of public officials, while the Puritans took over the supervision of the citizen. One could not expect a society to
rise above the moral level of its members. And if they were
to attain the angelic heights, private citizens would have
to coöperate at home as well as at the polls. Puritans made
it their special province to keep wayward individuals——
the drunkards, the prostitutes, and the sensualists—from
falling out of line. If their program as preached during the
Gilded Age had succeeded, the whole community would
have become a New Jerusalem with uprightness and integrity prevailing in our public life and sobriety and restraint
prevailing in our private life.

Now this was not altogether such a meddlesome business
as it might seem today. Vice was widespread among the
submerged members of the population; chronic drinking
among men and prostitution among women provided temporary escape rather then solutions for their problems. It
weakened their ardor for personal improvement and rendered
them slaves to their circumstances. When the reformers
concentrated upon the economic causes of vice rather than
on its moral aspects they often did fruitful work, as

with the agitation for fair working standards for women as an approach to the problem of prostitution. But on the whole, the Puritan emphasis was futile. The attempt to eradicate such vice through manipulation of the terrors of Hell was an enormous waste of energy. At the time the Puritan wing had achieved its great triumph in the Prohibition Amendment, Harold Stearns came to the conclusion that there was little hope for progressivism unless it was saved from its dour companion.

> "I have dwelt on this tradition of enforced morality because it has colored and shaped so many of the reform movements in the United States and because it is in no sense a part of the tradition of American liberalism. On the contrary, as we have seen in the specific case of prohibition, the liberals themselves have been intimidated by it or apathetic toward it. Indeed, it is exactly this perverted Puritanism, together with the heritage of race-hatred psychology that have made the development of a vital and influential American liberalism so extraordinarily difficult. Both heritages have worked for intolerance and coercion."[1]

2. THE PURITAN WING

In 1862 the United States Brewers' Association was formed to defend the trade against Puritan onslaughts. Its pressure proved so effective in both major parties that the prohibitionists resolved they could proceed no further without a party of their own, which they formed in 1869. In its early platforms this Prohibitionist Party was broadly and consistently progressive, advocating currency reform, direct election of the President, Vice President and Senators, lower railroad rates, civil service reform, woman suffrage and the curbing of monopolies. Its progressive leanings proved disastrous, however, many prohibitionists having been lured to the Populist movement in 1892 and still others succumbing to the free silver appeal of William Jennings Bryan in 1896.

It was the Anti-Saloon League, operating under a different strategy, that was the most effective vehicle for prohibition. Founded as the Local Option League in Ohio in 1888, this group began to work for local reforms in the counties and in the states by playing one party off against another. Slowly but surely, they secured the passage of anti-liquor laws throughout the country. In 1910 William Allen White, in summing up the achievements of the progressive movement of the decade, had much praise for the Puritan wing. For, he said, in the struggle against the corporate power the liquor interests were a mighty obstacle; and if the railroad reformers, the utility reformers, the oil reformers had all been as successful in their fight as the liquor reformers, surely capitalism would be on its last legs.

Throughout its history the movement for woman suffrage went side by side with the prohibition movement. They made the same slow progress among the states, went into a national drive together in 1913, and finally rode to victory on a wave of World War hysteria in the same year, 1920.

I might have included my comment on the struggle for woman's rights in the previous chapter as an example of extension of political democracy. As the country became more and more industrialized, women began to play an increasingly important rôle in the economy while denied the legal rights, the suffrage, and the bargaining power of men. From the strategic point of view it had been extremely difficult to balance the scales.

Great as was the contribution of the feminists to the cause of democratization, they contributed even more to the Puritan wing. For they minced no words as to where they stood on the liquor question. In 1874 there had been a mass revolt among the good women of Ohio. They put on demonstrations of Bible singing in the streets and saloons of the small towns. They formed the Women's Christian

Temperance Union, which, under the able leadership of Frances Willard, became one of the most powerful woman's organizations in the world. Indeed, when the W.C.T.U. demanded the vote, one might very well have predicted that the American government would soon be at the mercy of a great, aggressive Puritan army. Carrie Chapman Catt explains:

> "It was doubtless because of these things [the W.C.T.U. riots] that the press reports of the Brewers' Convention of 1881 included the account of the adoption of an anti-suffrage resolution to the effect that the Brewers would welcome prohibition as less dangerous to the trade than woman suffrage, because prohibition could be repealed at any time but woman suffrage would ensure the permanency of prohibition."[2]

The Puritan wing had many other preoccupations besides the bottle. They were concerned, for example, with organized vice. Most of the municipal reform movements in the 1890's and the 1900's were directed as much at the connection between the city bosses and the prostitutes as at the connection between the city bosses and the street railways. The Rev. Dr. Charles Parkhurst of New York was only the most conspicuous of many vice crusaders. And it was the exception rather than the rule when Mayor Tom L. Johnson decided that if he had to choose between moral and economic reform in the city of Cleveland, he would rather choose the economic. Lincoln Steffens wrote approvingly of him:

> "He gave vice that privilege [of breaking the law] for the price of quiet and non-interference with his police force, to get rid of them in order that he, as a business man, might as mayor deal with the corruption which he did understand."[3]

There was an increase of all kinds of prudish agitations and blue laws. There was, for example, the Anti-Profanity League, founded in 1903, whose members presented every blasphemer with the handbill, stating "Biting Satan's bare hook! Swearing satisfies no desire, gives no pleasure, makes no one happier, wiser, or better." The league flourished for a while, claimed 12,000 members, received the endorsement of Theodore Roosevelt and the Archbishop of Canterbury, and finally secured anti-swearing ordinances at Hanson, Massachusetts and at Tekemah, Nebraska.

What is even more surprising is that the progressive intellectuals in large part favored the Puritan association. Indeed, the English Fabians in arguing against capitalism maintained that it not only deprived the workers of the fruit of their toil, but that it made it impossible for them to lead Christian and moral lives. This was true at the summit as well as at the base of social life. The topmost members of society, relieved of the necessity of earning a living, sank into a torpor characterized by idleness, lying and hypocrisy. Such workers as came into the service of the rich, dressmakers, chauffeurs, and butlers, were affected with the poison and themselves became snobbish and dehumanized. Meanwhile, the great mass of productive labor took no pride in their work. Without leisure or education they acquired coarse habits and took to gambling and drinking. Most wretched of all were the unskilled and the unemployed who were on the verge of complete ostracism. In time they and their families were reduced to beggary, thievery, and prostitution.

Thus the Socialists at the turn of the century showed that a good Puritan must necessarily be a Socialist; for capitalism was the greatest vice of all and left a trail of lesser vices in the course of its depradation. Upton Sinclair's crusading novel, *The Jungle*, was much in this tradition. He gave a grueling picture of capitalist exploitation in the Chicago stockyards. There was tragedy enough in the economic hardships of his hero, in the conditions in the packing houses, in the extortions of the real estate agents, and in the problems of securing food and fuel. But for Sinclair these were not the crowning indignities of capitalism. They only became manifest with the moral degeneration of the Lithuanian peasant family, when the hero took to drink and when one of the hero's relatives became a prostitute. Indeed a contemporary critic pointed out that the portion of the novel dealing with the life of the prostitute was so vivid that the author must have spent most of his time at research in the Chicago brothels. This charge made Sinclair furious and he wrote a letter to the critic declaring that he had never entered a brothel in his life. Sinclair retained this Puritan conscience ever after and even added vegetarianism to his many interests.

On the whole, I say, this association with Puritanism was enervating and did much harm to the cause. By the time of the Prohibition Amendment the intellectuals of *The Nation* and *The New Republic* began to feel the contradictions of their position, which showed them a little absurd *vis à vis* the bar of civilization. Harold Stearns vividly described their plight:

> "American liberals are, on the whole, a rather bloodless lot and on Armistice Day—or rather on the more spontaneous mistaken Thursday previous I fancy very few of them were to be found reeling through the streets of New York or even fighting for a chance to buy a holiday cocktail. There is a kind of YMCA background to their mind; there is a touch of the Chautauqua in them; they are just a trifle too self-consciously good and pure. The ordinary man who, like the ordinary man of all ages, preserves something of the healthy Rabelaisian subsoil in him is usually a trifle embarassed in talking with them, as a street-walker might be embarassed in her first encounter with an angel. Of course this is the more or less natural result of the American tradition which instinctively couples virtue with abnegation and restraint instead of identifying it with activity and fighting for certain good ends. Yet it is a real pity, for it has

in the popular mind tended to bring discredit upon all 'reformers'. . . . The self-consciously liberal journals of New
York, such as *The New Republic, The Nation, The Dial, The
Public,* and the *Survey,* confined their notice of the prohibition
campaign to polite gibes at its absurdity when indeed they con-
descended to notice it at all. Yet coercion for the sake of virtue
is as repugnant as coercion for the sake of vice. If American
liberals are unwilling to fight the principle of coercion in the case
of the Prohibition Amendment simply because they are not
much interested in whether the country is dry or not, then they
are discredited the moment they fight coercion in those cases
where they *are* interested."[4]

3. PURITANS IN DECLINE

During the decade of the 1920's progressive activity sank
into the doldrums and intellectual life was, on the whole,
centered upon the attempt to introduce a measure of civilization into the folkways of our Puritan-ridden, provincial
America. We turned from the problem of how to distribute
wealth to the more neglected problem of how to employ
what we had; and political discussions became permeated
with such issues as the merits of Prohibition, the Ku Klux
Klan, with emphasis not only on its racial problem, but
on its cultural tensions between rural and urban America,
the attack on civil liberties with the threat to intellectual
liberty, censorship of "immoral" literature, and so forth.

The Puritan wing of the progressive movement became a
great liability, and the contradictions within the cause became manifest. For if redistribution of income led to
greater political civilization, how was it possible to stomach
the Puritans who would check any further progress towards
cultural civilization? H. L. Mencken, among others, could
not see that a reconciliation was possible; and he moved on
to attack democracy as fundamentally decivilizing and unfit
as a harbor for the arts and sciences.

The case for Puritan progressivism was demonstrated *ad*

absurdum by William Jennings Bryan at the monkey trial in Tennessee. It was indeed dramatic that the one man who in his youth had captured the leadership of the progressive cause by his Puritanical fervor, should have reduced that cause to its most ridiculous terms when virtually on his death-bed. He was the rare combination of a Sir Galahad in his youth and a Don Quixote in his senescence, and he was superb in both rôles. For Bryan was perhaps the best demonstration of how the Puritan strain got mixed up with the progressive, and of how disastrous was the combination. As a youth he seems to have shared his time equally between reading the Bible and attacking Wall Street, and he often gave sermons at a political rally and political harangues at Chautauqua. Take, for example, his mighty "cross of gold" speech at the Democratic Convention in 1896. It was shot through with religious imagery and phraseology. Indeed he derived most of his lyrical power by translating the conflict over the free coinage of silver into the conflict of Jesus with the infidels:

> "The humblest citizen in all the land, when clad in the armor of a righteous cause, is stronger than all the hosts of error. I come to speak to you in defense of a cause as holy as the cause of liberty—the cause of humanity. Having behind us the producing masses of this nation and the world, supported by the commercial interest, the laboring interests, and the toilers everywhere, we will answer their demand for a gold standard by saying to them: *You shall not press down upon the brow of labor this crown of thorns, you shall not crucify mankind upon a cross of gold.*"

This confusion was already becoming outmoded when Bryan took his place as Secretary of State in Wilson's Cabinet—when he insisted on the right to preach the evils of drink and temptation at Chautauqua and when he was conducting his grape-juice diplomacy with the civilized

countries of the world.   The transition from Galahad to
Quixote was by then well under way.   The press generally
held him up as a comic figure far removed from the revolutionary menace of 1896, and John Reed, who later died
in Moscow, wrote a full account of his taste in the arts and
literature for the delectation of the enlightened.

But it was his final tilt with the windmill of evolution that
finished him figuratively and literally.   As is well-known,
Mr. Scopes was brought to book under a Tennessee statute
that forbade the teaching of the Darwinian Theory of
Evolution in state schools.   Clarence Darrow defended the
accused, Bryan upheld the state, and H. L. Mencken did
the reporting.   This time the cards were obviously all on
the side of civilization.   Bryan was reduced to defending
the Biblical account of the founding of the universe and
the Natural Order.   And millions of farmers, valiant crusaders for free silver, turned over in their graves at the
humiliation of their erstwhile leader.

With the advent of the New Deal we have shaken off the
weight of Puritan encumbrances.   We began with good omen
when the lame-duck Congress on February 20, 1933, ap-
proved the Twenty-First Amendment repealing enforced
morality from our fundamental law, and when the New
Deal Congress on March 22, legalized 3.2% beer.   Rexford
Tugwell in a rather remarkable statement expressed the
hope for a civilized progressivism.

> "It would be treason to the entire spirit of the New Deal to lose
> sight of the fact that its objective, as stated by President
> Roosevelt himself is to make possible a more abundant life for
> the American people . . . the enjoyment of the good things of
> life in security and contentment, and the cultivation, through
> such enjoyment of the good things of the spirit.
>
> "The women of this country have a great opportunity to
> establish and maintain a civilized attitude towards wine now that
> we have all seen what comes of not cultivating such a civilized

attitude. . . . If they follow the old line, they can drive their men back to the barroom and the short stiff drinks which go with the barroom. If they follow a new and more civilized line, they can accompany their men to the cafes and beer gardens and consume at leisure the long, slow drinks which are appropriate to pleasant conversations and mature social relationships.

"You may wonder why I, as an official of the Department of Agriculture, should concern myself with the drinking habits of the American people. . . ."[5]

Perhaps Mr. Tugwell, as an official of the Department of Agriculture, spoke more for the interest of American wine producers than for the improvement of American civilization, and unquestionably, the liquor lobby had much to do with the Repeal. Nonetheless, the emancipation of the New Deal has persisted. It is best symbolized by the First Family. Theodore Roosevelt, for all his strenuousness, was rather prim and upright in his domestic habits. H. G. Wells, in *The New Machiavelli* (1910), spoke of the "badtemper" of T. R.'s Administration, due partly to the rigid standards of trust-busting as explained in the preceding chapters, and partly to an excessive concern for the private morality of the American people.

The present representatives of the clan in office are built on more generous lines. Mrs. Roosevelt is a militant champion of the independent and civic-minded woman. She believes in a civilized attitude towards the vices. She has pleaded for moderate drinking and for dissolution of marriage ties in cases of incompatibility. And her sprawling and far-flung family has practiced these precepts before the eyes of the country. And yet, by its very nature, the present moral temper is more conspicuous by the absence of the Puritans than by overt expressions on the part of the administration. The new attitude is not evangelical. Nor can it be expressed in government, except by abandoning the invasion of domestic privacy. When the Puritans withdrew from the progressive movement there were no new censors to take their place.

4. WILL THEY COME BACK?

It would be wrong to think that Puritanism has completely vanished from the scene. When John L. Lewis characterized Vice-President Garner as a "poker-playing, whiskey-drinking, evil old man," he was no doubt carefully calculating his remark to appeal to the moral prejudices of the working people. And Maury Maverick, one of the staunchest New Dealers both in Congress and as Mayor of San Antonio, has expressed his resentment at New York intellectualism, all of which savors of the blue-nose.

> "All the time I have been going to New York I have been eating up 'plays', drama, and culture, until Eugene O'Neill wrote a five-and-a-half hour play. Then it seemed time to revolt against all this intellect. I got the idea then, and the idea is fixed now, that to spend hours and hours on the particular life of a single person, especially of one who is an isolated psychopath and not representive of the people as a whole, is wasted time. That applies to books as well."[6]

There is good reason to believe that the emancipation from Puritanism never really penetrated the hinterland. For example, the progressivism of the Middle West, of Wisconsin, Minnesota, and North Dakota, still retains many Populist characteristics. We have frequently been reminded of the greater virtue and greater militancy of this section over other sections of the country. Progressives in less advanced states have badgered themselves, "Why aren't we like Wisconsin?" or "Why aren't we like Minnesota?" And when the elder La Follette went visiting in the Soviet Union he told Lenin that the Communists could learn a great deal from the Wisconsin experiment.

Since Utopia is so very near and since there are not many ages which can boast of perfection within an overnight train ride, instead of on some far-off planet, or on some hitherto unexplored area of the globe, I resolved to set out at once. I resolved to visit Milwaukee, until recently the Socialist stronghold which is set in the heart of Progressive Wisconsin.

I went down to City Hall—the old *Ratshaus* with its Germanic towers and ramparts—Capitol of American Socialism. The Mayor himself was out of town but his assistant offered to answer my inquiries as to how a Socialist ran a great metropolis.

"Look at Jersey City," he said, "and then you will understand. In 1936 we had a small *per capita* debt of $90 while they had one of $254. We charged a mild *per capita* tax on property of $50, while they charged $81. We had reduced our debt by $4,600,000; they had increased theirs by $4,800,000. In short, we are economical.

"Nor did we stint on services." And he proceeded with more statistics on the material charms of life in Milwaukee. "There you have it. The difference between a Fascist America and a Socialist America. We've got them beat in every way."

"But," I asked, "is the difference simply one of dollars and cents?"

"Well," he replied, "there is a hygienic difference too. We are clean. We have the healthiest city in the country. We have an ordinance preventing the distribution of leaflets in the streets. Do you know why? Simply because they inevitably get down the drains and clog up our sewers. And that would never do, for a free-flowing sewer is the very backbone of any healthy city, not to mention a Socialist city.

"And we have gone even further. We are now in the

midst of a campaign to prevent spitting. You have no idea how unsanitary it is."

I remarked that I had seen large painted letters on the sidewalks, "Don't spit on the Sidewalk." "But still," I said, "I don't see the essential Socialism. Don't you try to redistribute wealth, foster class feeling, and encourage agitators with grants of civil liberties?"

"Of course, of course," he said, waving these things aside as so much routine. "Take the ordinary capitalist city— Chicago, Boston, Baltimore. When people want recreation they go into cheap dance halls. They go out to unprotected bathing resorts or to dark parks where all kinds of nonsense goes on. But come to a Socialist city like Milwaukee. Do we let our citizens degenerate like that? Certainly not! We take responsibility not only for the city's business, but for the city's pleasure as well. We supply them with public dance halls and with bathing beaches—both carefully supervised. And as to our parks, you will not find a square foot of space after sundown that is not perfectly illuminated and well-patroled.

"Besides, we close all our facilities at 11 P.M. You see the voters here look to us to protect their children. And if we don't see that all the young folks get back to their homes before midnight, we get angry calls from the parents here at City Hall and down there at police headquarters."

I thanked the Mayor's assistant for the interview. But I went away feeling that there was certainly more of Queen Victoria in his administration than of Nicolai Lenin.

Now it may well be that we can never outlive the Puritans and that we are living in the shadow of the moral liberation of the 1920's and of the collapse of Bryanism. It is very possible, as H. L. Mencken argues, that there is a fundamental connection between prudery in personal morality and democracy in the conduct of public affairs, and that both are antagonistic to the niceties of civilization. As he wrote in *Notes on Democracy* (1926):

> "A glance at it [democratic law] is sufficient to show the identity of democracy and Puritanism. The two indeed, are but different facets of the same gem. In the psyche they are one. For both get their primal essence out of the inferior man's fear and hatred of his betters."[7]

It may well be true. The arts and vices of civilization that delight surfeited bankers may be enervating for the rebellious masses. It may be good policy for every progressive movement to retain its Puritan wing so that its members will be disciplined and attentive to the woes of the world. I hope not. For however logical this policy may be, I earnestly hope that the progressivism of the future can proceed on the enlightened level that has been established over the last eight years.

Part III

DEFLATION IN ECONOMIC POLICY

CHAPTER SIX

The New Strategy

1. Another Age of Heroes
2. Why Borah Was An Enigma
3. End of Emancipation

I. ANOTHER AGE OF HEROES

SINCE the First World War we have been living in a new Age of Heroes. Millions of human beings in various countries of the Western World, finding their personal problems insoluble, have turned themselves over to secular leaders and endowed them with super-human potency. The rise of hero-worship is not confined to the Fascist and Communist powers. It is also evident in the American democracy with the prolonged and unprecedented popularity of President Roosevelt and in the British democracy with the emergence of Winston Churchill; and if it was less evident in the last days of France, its very absence may have contributed to her final collapse. Naturally we differ as to the way we expect our hero to solve our problems. But the fact remains that increasingly the major decisions in our lives as to our profession, our manner of living, and our antipathies are made, and will be made, not by us as individuals, but by us as members of the entourage of a hero.

Progressives may resent hero-worship in other lands, yet inevitably they have been employing it for their own purposes at home. This change reflects a striking shift in strategy. Until recently, progressives had been doing everything in their power to hamper and bind the hero. And they had been gloriously successful. They had extinguished such human dinosaurs as Charles V, Henry VIII, James I and Louis XIV who roamed over Europe in the Jurassic Age of the sixteenth and seventeenth centuries. Now they are helping to conjure them up again. They are subverting all their mighty works. It is a consummation of terrible irony!

What had been accomplished was the tearing down of governmental authority and the setting up of the free and equal individual. This was the Liberal Idea; and now that we are abandoning the old strategy, we can set its dates roughly from the Great Rebellion in England in the middle of the seventeenth century to the Treaty of Versailles at the end of the First World War. The strategy was slow and uncertain. Gradually the heroes gave way before a triumphant Parliament in England, a wild and bloody revolution in France, and a colonial rebellion in America. Now and again there were reverses as in the rise of Napoleon I, part anachronism and part anticipation, as in the rise of his nephew, Napoleon III, and of Andrew Jackson and Abraham Lincoln. These men were caught in the interval between two heroic ages. They had lonely reputations in a world where mediocrity was both desired and acclaimed.

The liberal spirit was corrosive of all pretensions of overweening authority. It questioned all claims of a mystical nature and demanded that, if these were to be maintained, they must be restated in rational terms. Thus the figures of public life became suspect. Strong men could no longer disport under the guise of a dispensation from God as did Charles I. It was not enough that he was descended, as his supporters claimed, from a line of kings going back to old Adam. The private citizen, the Common Individual was at the basis of all liberal policy. And through him kings, once masters of all they surveyed, were transformed into the people's servants.

If the liberal strategy succeeded in doing away with political despots, it had less fortunate results in the economic realm. There it was designed to free the individual enterpriser from the restraints of mercantile law and, in general, from governmental interference. But, as the nineteenth century wore on, the anticipations of social harmony failed to materialize. Out of the free market came, not harmony, but the rise of the most able and shrewd enterprisers—a new breed of despots, who, by their position in the production and distribution of goods, held power over the wages of thousands of workers and the prices of the stuff of life for millions of consumers. They were adventurers mounted on such chargers as had never been seen before—railroads, steamboats, telegraphs, manufactures with all kinds of technical innovations. Nor was there any law to ensure that the chargers would be ridden in accordance with social well-being.

When the facts of economic despotism finally reached the mass consciousness in the United States in the 1890's and 1900's, it was only natural that the progressives—the agrarians and trust-busters—should resort to the same strategy by which their liberal forefathers had overthrown political despotism one hundred years before. They appealed to the practise of Thomas Jefferson who had best represented the Liberal Idea in America. They cried out that the Robber Barons of industry, like the Stuart Kings of England and the Bourbons of France, had violated the basic assumptions upon which society was founded, and that the common man, this time the farmer and the small business man, must reassert himself.

The technique of anti-trust agitation was fundamentally

the technique of liberal revolution. The trust, the economic despot, must be overthrown by being broken down into the components of economic life, the small individual producers. Hence we find the Sherman Anti-Trust Act of 1890 as the economic equivalent of the guillotine that chopped off the head of Louis XVI. Just as the old liberals recognized the need for some form of government, and in constituting such a government hedged it around with the most elaborate restrictions, so too the anti-trust agitators recognized the need for some large corporations, particularly in the field of railroads and public utilities. And they too devised regulatory devices to ensure that their powers would not be abused.

2. WHY BORAH WAS AN ENIGMA

Whereas absolute monarchy had become outmoded and obsolete in the seventeenth and eighteenth centuries and was ripe for dissolution, the institutions of monopoly capitalism were far from obsolete at the beginning of the twentieth century. They had become an integral part of our productive processes, and the strategy of dissolution, of trust-busting, was unavailing against them. Slowly we are coming to realize this. Capitalism lies in our midst like the fire of Prometheus, handed down, not by the gods, but by human ingenuity in the nineteenth century, and we have become so dependent upon it that we are powerless to blow it out.

This fire has been badly employed in private hands, flaring up occasionally into a conflagration that spreads havoc throughout the community. And even when it is under control, its warmth is neither widely nor equitably shared. The progressives have reluctantly come to the conviction that they must take over its management themselves. They will become masters of the flames.

Here is the paradox, that it is necessary to recreate the old bogy of political despotism in order to destroy the new bogy of economic despotism. This was something that Thomas Jefferson with his liberal prejudices had not bargained for. The latterday Jeffersonians like William Jennings Bryan wavered uneasily between the old-fashioned state rights, on one hand, and on the other, the new necessity for government ownership of railroads which would have involved centralization of power diametrically opposed to state rights. Woodrow Wilson, who proclaimed in a campaign speech in 1912 that "the history of liberty is a history of the limitation of governmental power, not the increase of it", became the sponsor of the Federal Reserve System which concentrated control over credit facilities and, later, became the administrator of our war-time collectivism.

Herbert Croly, one of the earliest effective exponents of the collectivist line, was well aware of the paradox. In the "constructive national democracy" which he outlined in 1908, he proposed adoption of the Hamiltonian strategy, the creation of a strong central government, in order to achieve Jeffersonian ends, the extension of economic and political democracy. In his words, "the national government must step in and discriminate; but it must discriminate not on behalf of liberty and the special individual, but on behalf of equality and the average man."[1] Croly warned that we would have to give up the Jeffersonian strategy. The fear of a strong federal government and the hope of grappling with economic problems through state governments, which were safeguards of democracy in an agrarian society, had become obstacles to democracy in a highly developed industrial society.

Yet we adjusted ourselves slowly. We have been hesitant to discard the old strategy. Obsolescence overtook those progressives who refused to accept the deflation in moral content. Again obsolescence is overtaking progressives who refuse to accept deflation in economic policy. At every advance towards collectivism and centralized control these men raise the outmoded cry of state rights, and their supporters become at first puzzled, then suspicious, and finally bitter.

Senator William E. Borah experienced all these reactions. He was regarded variously as an enigma, a man of paradoxes, unpredictable and unclassifiable, perverse, or even opportunistic. Yet part of the enigma can be explained, I believe, by the fact that he was overtaken by obsolescence at an early age, and yet concealed the true state of his decay by an extremely long and vocal life and by his very forceful public expressions.

Carter Glass once said that Borah was the greatest exponent of state rights in his day. Pronounced by a Virginia Democrat about a Far Western Republican, the judgment must have carried great weight. It was true, I believe, to this extent: the tenacious belief in state rights caused more contradictions in the career of Senator Borah than in that of any other self-styled and probably sincere progressive of the era. For if there was one thread of consistency throughout, it was this rigid Constitutional doctrine around which hung those inhibiting fears of federal power.

When Borah first appeared in the Senate, under the mild reforms of Theodore Roosevelt's Square Deal and of the Taft administration, there was no apparent contradiction, and it has been generally agreed that Borah was more at home in the progressive movement at that time than ever after. Even then he had expressed opposition to T. R.'s conservation program when it worked hardship on the economic development of Idaho and had suggested that conservation was properly the province of the states.

Moreover when T. R. expounded his New Nationalism program for the control and supervision of the trusts rather than their annihilation and formed the Bull Moose party in 1912, Borah made it quite clear that though he sympathized with the Rough Rider personally, he could not accept his program.

He refused to support the federal amendment for woman's suffrage, but at the same time, he supported the federal prohibition amendment. When the suffragettes protested that he was inconsistent, he replied very neatly that suffrage could come in one state without being jeopardized by the absence of suffrage in another, but that prohibition, through the difficulty of controlling the liquor traffic, could only be established on a federal basis.

During the New Freedom and after, while still flying the progressive flag, Borah became more and more obstructive, and gradually assumed the proportions of the most enigmatical man in public life. Defiantly he declared that federal control of wages and hours, child labor, and education was unconstitutional. He opposed the setting up of the Federal Trade Commission in 1914 on the grounds that it would put too much discretion in the hands of a federal bureau. He opposed the federal anti-lynching bills. And he opposed Senate approval of the Child Labor Amendment in 1924. By this time, progressive groups in the country were getting rather irked with their stalwart, but outmoded, champion. But the Lion remained firm. In reply to a critic he wrote:

> "I regard it [the Child Labor Amendment] as the most pronounced invasion of local self-government that has ever been proposed. I think it changes the whole structure of our government. We place 40,000,000 human beings under the absolute control of Congress. And all this seems to be so utterly unnecessary in view of the fact that only two states now really are behind in child labor legislation."[2]

After some twenty years of this tantalizing performance, we could well anticipate Borah's reaction to the New Deal. Even during the emergency period Borah opposed the major devices, the NRA, the first AAA, the cotton control, the Guffey Coal Act, and the Reciprocal Trade Act. And he was shocked continuously by excessive delegations of power to the President, by assaults on state rights, and by the general tendency towards centralization in Washington.

3. END OF EMANCIPATION

Although the collectivists talk of the great day of taking over, such event may carry with it some disadvantages. For though that day will be marked with material benefits for its participants, the necessities of collectivism require that they be organized and obedient to a highly centralized control. Just as the German people have submitted to what Hitler hopes will be a permanent dictatorship, so the progressives are slowly submitting themselves to a permanent organization in which the individual has little freedom, dignity or importance except in so far as he does his duty by his fellows.

Under the old strategy of individual emancipation, the horizons of human betterment seemed infinite, and with the increasing freedom of democracy, it seemed that mankind would become increasingly angelic. In the collectivist program such ascension is indefinitely postponed. As far as anyone knows, his soul will be unaltered. As things now stand, many citizens are sub-men, deficient in the full animal complement of food, clothing and shelter. In the day of collectivist triumph their animal wants presumably will be satisfied. It will be simply a rearrangement of the existing factors in the economy so as to distribute wider satisfaction. There is little hope of a higher humanity with a greater endowment of goodness and benevolence emerging in the process.

This, indeed, is the most important aspect of the deflation of American ideals. It is most clearly seen, I think, in the changed character of political education. We no longer care to develop the individual as a unique contributor to a democratic form. We want him as a private in an army, cooperating with all the other privates. The old Jeffersonian emphasis on schools for citizenship and on self-government has changed to a Rooseveltian emphasis on response to a heroic leadership.

President Roosevelt has prided himself on the amount of discussion that he has provoked and on the thorough grounding in political and economic fundamentals that he has given the voters in the pursuance of his program. And yet he is palpably more interested in having them consent to and participate in his *faits accomplis* than in having them share in the preliminary deliberations. As an educator, he has disseminated the facts, because the facts have been mainly on his side. On the other hand, he is no more interested in stimulating strategic thought among the citizens than the General Staff of the U. S. Army is interested in stimulating strategic thought among the soldiers.

I do not think that this change in educational policy is anything to glory in. Yet it is essential. If it seems to undermine the dignity of the common man, it is because his dignity has already been undermined. The progressives are not the ones who did it. The great factories which take in raw materials at one end and turn out complicated mechanisms at the other end of the assembly line and which involve the total labor of millions of men, have distorted the Jeffersonian dream. We have been turned into a nation with super-men, oligarchs, exercising enormous powers over the jobs, working conditions, and standards of living of the great masses of sub-men, the workers. The collectivists have adopted the strategy of uniting these sub-men in order to challenge the super-men more effectively. In this movement each individual sub-man is important, not for his uniqueness, but for his ability to lose himself in the mass, through his fidelity to the trade union, or cooperative organization, or political party.

Do you weep for the death of the common man? It will do no good. He is dead and it is much more important to save the sub-men who have taken his place, by the strategy that I have here outlined. Besides, those who shed the most tears at this deflation of a glorious American ideal are those who are most responsible for it—namely, the business community. By insisting on reviving the image of the Jeffersonian common man, they are only preventing the industrial sub-man from ever sharing in the fruits of his toil; and they are tantalizing him with an antique and futile dream.

We must rebuild strong governmental institutions once more. Instead of an attitude of hostility, we must have an attitude of respect towards the claims of political power. We must form ourselves into a solid progressive army behind our heroes. For the new collectivist devices do not operate by themselves, as did the laws of free competition. In the next chapter I shall suggest to what degree the Roosevelt administration has organized an army of occupation to take over this new control.

CHAPTER SEVEN
Roosevelt as Hero

1. Ethical Revolution
2. The Battlefield
3. The Progressive Army
4. Independent Battalions
5. Communications
6. Dynamics of Heroism

1. ETHICAL REVOLUTION

IT HAS been tacitly recognized that the progressives in America are undergoing an ethical revolution which in the history of their movement will play the same part as the Counter Reformation in the Catholic Church. There is as much difference between a neo-progressive like Max Lerner and a paleo-progressive like his former colleague, Oswald Garrison Villard, as there is between St. Ignatius and St. Francis. Editors of *The New York Times* and the *New York Herald Tribune*, who have themselves never been in the forefront of the progressive fight, have made lament for the change in values. They have said, in effect, "We could at least find spiritual stimulus in Mr. Villard; we find nothing but will to power in Mr. Lerner." Whether they call it will to power, militancy, realism, or even cynicism, it is evident that a change has taken place.

What has happened? Faced with enemies that are full of fraud and violence, the progressives have given up trying to evangelize them and have come around to adopting some of their own devices. In a gangster world they have employed a tough leader and stocked up a few sub-machine guns of their own. This is a weighty decision. For if progressives adopt the high-handed methods of their opponents, what is left to distinguish them? What will ensure the survival of their noble ends in a morass of ignoble means? For is there not a basic inconsistency between a strategy of power and the democratic ideal?

These questions were most dramatically posed by the actions of the New Deal administration in its era of reform. Then we saw a progressive government attempt to concentrate power in its own hands, not in imitation of its reactionary predecessors, but rather in an effort to defend popular interests against the subtle power of the corporations.

An economic despotism had grown up in the shelter of this free country. It was an almost invulnerable stronghold, entrenched behind barricades of newspapers, political hirelings without number, and vast resources for confusing and frustrating the public. What we needed was a progressive army with comparable political power, with full equipment for defense and counter-attack. If they had holding companies, we must have trade unions. If they suppressed some of our civil liberties, we must suppress some of theirs. If they had their political hirelings in the Republican Party, we must secure ours in the Democratic Party. And if they had fought wars in the interest of American imperialism, we should fight ours in the interest of progressive survival against Fascism (although perhaps we could both manage to get satisfaction out of the same war).

But the struggle was difficult. Let the President try to endow an administrative agency with the price-fixing powers long held by private citizens, and every voter trembles with fear. "A strong leader in a strong government! What will become of our liberties?" they cried. It was needless to argue that such power was only a defensive action in the public interest against a terrible monster. No, the burden of proof has always been on the government, especially a progressive government. It was only in the extremity of the depression and the bank crisis that the President could obtain enough constitutional authority to meet the monster on somewhat equal terms.

With the assumption of power by the progressives, they could at last enjoy some of that proud assurance that the conservatives enjoyed for so many years. Back in the 1870's and the 1880's the business magnates were on the offensive, the railroad builders, the oil refiners,—the Hills and Harrimans, the Cookes and the Rockefellers. Then William H. Vanderbilt could declare flippantly, "The public be damned."

Now it was the public's turn to be flippant at the expense of the business community. Mr. Roosevelt, for example, discussing the merits of his Court Plan a few years after its rejection, pointed out that though he failed to achieve that particular reform, nevertheless he had changed the attitude of the court and had indirectly achieved his purpose. "The country is naturally concerned with the attainment of proper objectives rather than any one of many possible methods proposed for the accomplishment of that end," he said. To which the *New York Herald-Tribune* replied in horror, "The highwayman's method he proposed was the whole issue. Is it possible that he doesn't yet understand this? Does he still think the country believes with him that the end justifies the means?"[1]

Old progressives do not relish this new temper any more than its conservative victims. William Allen White, in

The Old Order Changeth (1910), laid down what was generally accepted as sound progressive strategy when he declared that the struggle over capitalism must be fought out within each man's heart.   Monopoly capitalism, he felt, was largely a wave of evil that could be exorcised by preaching.   The progressive forces should be organized as though they were a spiritual congregation—that is, not by pitting the workers and farmers against the capitalists, but by urging everybody to fight the temptation to become a capitalist.   And he warned:

> "Those who teach democracy the doctrine of an eye for an eye and a tooth for a tooth, even against those who have oppressed the people, they are democracy's foes."[2]

This appeal was not wholly without success.   A few capitalists became deeply disturbed by their evil role in American life and turned to reform.   Indeed, the spectacle of the various millionaire reformers was one of the many remarkable ones of the Progressive Era: Tom L. Johnson, utility magnate, turned reform Mayor of Cleveland; Samuel Fels, the soap manufacturer, with his endowments for the propagation of Henry George's single tax theory; Edward Filene, the Boston merchant, offering to turn his department store over to his employees; and Mrs. Willard Straight with her benefactions to *The New Republic*.

But, on the whole, it was a fruitless crusade.   The progressives had grossly underestimated the attractions of capitalism for those who prospered under it, even more than Christianity underestimated the attractiveness of sin. For while sin often enters our lives as a luxury, capitalism had entered our lives as a sheer necessity for the distribution of material goods.   And we have arrived at the point where our domestic progress depends on the practise of that very doctrine, "an eye for an eye and a tooth for a tooth."

2. THE BATTLEFIELD

The progressives are no longer a lot of centrifugal atoms, changing society by flying off in revolt against authority. They are now submitting to organization, moving in one direction and loyal to a leader. They must eventually be able to take over and operate the corporate power as a kind of conquered province. Hence, from the ethical point of view, they have changed from a spiritual congregation into a military army. The ethics of military activity is simply group aggrandizement, and progressivism has become the aggrandizement of the majority groups at the expense of the minority.

Can you doubt that the progressives have adopted military ethics in everything but the use of violence? There is the division of society into a battlefield, not necessarily the Marxian battlefield of class warfare, but at least a battlefield with corporate power on one side and all the economic groups which feel its impact arrayed on the other. There are the leaders to whom obedience and loyalty are due. There are the tactical movements, with the progressive army in command of the government, and the conservative army in command of business markets and investments. And as the progressive army moves into the business domain, the conservative army replies in kind with its artillery division, the newspaper publishers, and with a graceful retreat from capital investment, which is like burning the wheat fields before the on-marching army so that it will be deprived of necessary supplies.

The military temper was especially clear in the progressive thrusts as of 1935 and again of 1937. It was never formulated into a rounded philosophy, but was indicated in a number of unmistakable signs: in President Roosevelt's Madison Square Garden speech of 1936 when he declared, "I should like to have it said of my first Administration that in it the forces of selfishness and of lust for power met their match.   I should like to have it said of my second Administration that in it these forces met their master"; in remarks, such as "We're going to tax and tax, spend and spend, elect and elect" attributed to Harry Hopkins; and "Fighting with a business man is like fighting with a Polack. You can give no quarter," attributed to Thomas G. Corcoran.   The latter remark is reported on the authority of Raymond Moley, who comments:

> "As I look back at this remark, it seems to epitomize much that has been wrong with the procedure of the lawyer-minded New Dealers of the past six years.   They see government operating successfully not through the process of consultation, compromise, and harmonious adjustment, but rather through the litigious process.   This implies that the art of government is a battle between the lawyers of the Lord and the lawyers of business. . . . In the end, these assumptions cannot help but create, as they have created, class feeling of the most intense sort."[3]

The business community in turn also expressed its resentment in military form, its war aim being comparable to that of the Americans in the First World War, with "That Man Roosevelt" replacing the Kaiser.

But perhaps the most important sign is the changing rôle of the political writer.   When politics was largely a struggle for the improvement of the human soul, writers were obviously preachers who appealed to their readers with the justice or injustice of the reform, and since the struggle was supposed to take place within the soul of every individual, writers were in the forefront of a spiritual struggle.

But in an economic struggle people know pretty well which side they are on by virtue of their stomachs and their pocketbooks.   It is as futile for Walter Lippmann to argue the steel workers' union into amending the Wagner Act

in the interest of his kind of social justice as it is futile for
The New Republic to argue the utilities into socialization
in the interest of their kind of social justice. You can
preach all you want, but at the end of your column your
audience will, on the whole, find its way into its own camp.
Political writers have now become army chaplains, bringing
sanctity to the warriors on their respective sides.

Yet the chaplain's is an humble role, and some writers, in
order to restore their prestige, have completely foresworn
the moral or persuasive functions of political writers.
Since our political life at home has become a struggle for
power between progressive and conservative forces, they
have set about the more serious and more military business
of planning strategy. Foremost in this school of writers is
Arthur Krock of *The New York Times*. Indeed, Krock is a
kind of self-constituted General Staff of conservatism in
America. For years he has been advising the conservatives
how they could most effectively embarrass the President.
He has been an ardent advocate of the anti-New Deal
Democratic and Republican coalition. He has known when
the Republicans should keep silent, how they could best
stir dissension within the Democratic ranks, and with
what issues they might best present themselves to the
public. For all his over-confidence, he is the new style
political observer *par excellence*. I believe that as time goes
on the Krocks will multiply on both sides and that, accordingly, the Thompsons and Lippmanns will dwindle.

3. THE PROGRESSIVE ARMY

During the Progressive Era leadership was more widely
diffused. Activity on the federal plane did not compare
with the intensity and boldness of activity in the states and
municipalities. In Wisconsin there was La Follette with
his Wisconsin Idea, and in Oregon the initiative and refer-

endum of John U'Ren. There were reform Governors like Hiram Johnson in California, Charles Evans Hughes in New York, Franklin Murphy and Woodrow Wilson in New Jersey; reform mayors like Samuel Jones in Toledo, Tom L. Johnson in Cleveland and Max Fagan in Jersey City. The ferment was equally alive in newspapers, magazines and churches. There was little danger that Theodore Roosevelt would outrun the tempo or enthusiasm of the country, but rather considerable evidence that he followed behind with a minimum of concession.

The New Deal, however, has pushed far ahead. There are occasional battalions of New Dealism in the hinterland: in California there were the unsuccessful campaign of Upton Sinclair and the successful one of Culbert Olson. Wisconsin and Minnesota have had a heritage of progressivism from pre-New Deal days. In New York City there is Mayor La Guardia. But on the whole, the initiative has come from Washington. The federal government has almost monopolized the motive power, the initiative and leadership of progressive spirit in America.

In the Progressive Era, with its moral concerns, there could be wide variety as to the vehicle of reform. Spiritual congregations could be formed anywhere, in cities or counties or states, and the introduction of upright methods was a forward step, no matter how small the unit of government. Organization for national action was sporadic and indecisive, and it was not until the New Deal with the more pressing demands for collective controls that this new strategy was put to the test.

But it is not enough that leadership be concentrated in Washington. There must be a following, an army with its devoted regiments and battalions in the hinterland. There must be popular support with which to overcome the institutional obstacles within the federal government—the recalcitrance of Congress and the Supreme Court. This army has only materialized very imperfectly; and time and again the General Staff has been left stranded in Washington, unable to make contact with the provincial units.

There are a number of reasons for this. First of all, President Roosevelt attempted to employ the party organization as the nucleus for a progressive army. He declared on numerous occasions that he wanted to make the Democratic Party a progressive party and that he wanted its candidates to represent that position before the American voters. Robert Jackson, now Attorney-General, advanced the equally remarkable thesis that a progressive Presidency must be measured not by its tenure of office but by its accomplishment in economic reform. And therefore, since much of the reform in F. D. R.'s first term was nullified by the courts, if he should run in 1940, it would be not for a third term, but really only for a second.

The Democratic Party has historically been a more effective vehicle for reform than its rival. Yet inevitably the New Dealers came squarely up against its conservative components, against the prejudices of southern Bourbons, of northern city machines, and of western mining interests. These elements in Congress rebelled against New Deal leadership. They hid behind the traditional separation of legislative and executive functions; and they raised the cry of dictatorship. Indeed, by 1937 there was more heat on the part of the internal opposition than from the outside. For some time the President had pampered these obstructionists. Now he proceeded to courtmartial them as traitors to the progressive cause. Hence the fateful attempt at a purge in 1938.

A political party consists, not only of a club on the national scale, but of local clubs in the states, cities and counties throughout the country. Although the President attempted to reform the federal officials, Senators and Congressmen, he hardly touched the local ones. These supported the Chief at elections, but were largely conservative, even reactionary in their localities. We had the remarkable spectacle of Mayor Hague of New Jersey, pleading loyalty to the New Deal and at the same time viciously interfering with the organization of the New Deal C.I.O. and of Mayor Kelly of Chicago, likewise pleading loyalty and yet allowing his police to shoot down striking steel workers in the Memorial Day massacre of 1937.

Curiously enough, while President Roosevelt failed to purge the party of its reactionary leaders, neither could the reactionary leaders purge him. By 1940 they were coming back to do him the honor of a third term nomination, like children returning home after a family tiff, not because they had been converted to progressivism, but because he was the only leader with sufficient stature to meet the new crisis and to carry their local tickets. For his third term the President still has nominal command over the Democratic Party, but the heritage of unreconstructed Bourbons is almost as formidable as before.

4. INDEPENDENT BATTALIONS

In their appeal to non-partisan voters and in their organization of independent battalions on an interest group basis, the New Dealers did much better. There is, of course, nothing new about the employment of interest groups in this way. For long they were employed on the other side. They were the battalions of business conservatism, of trade associations and manufacturers seeking special favors in the development of their industry, tariff benefits or subsidies of one kind or another. And their gratitude made them loyal supporters of the Republican army that had held Washington as a kind of semi-permanent camping ground since the Civil War.

Yet, inevitably, counter-interest groups on the progressive side have also existed, trade unions and reformist organizations. In the Progressive Era their function was grossly misunderstood. They were thought to be simply spiritual leaders who banded together for action out of exuberance and fervor. I quote again from William Allen White:

> "The important measures accomplished by the [Theodore] Roosevelt Administration . . . may be called the Roosevelt policies. Yet they are not his. He merely adopted them. He found in every case a strong parliamentary organization working for these things. . . .
>
> "Chief among the organizations propagating the right of people to industrial peace was and is the National Civic Federation. It is composed largely of rich men who have vision to see that they must surrender to the common good much of their vested rights, and generally these men find joy in it. Among other members of the Federation are labor leaders who see that they too and their constituents must give in before the common good and take joy in the giving. That sentiment is abroad in America today; it is the soul of our new-born democracy. So that one who looks at the large national movements of the decade now closing will find that those movements which have become national laws are laws looking to the distribution rather than the accumulation of wealth. Practically all the large national organizations which jam the trains annually going to their conventions are fundamentally altruistic. . . .
>
> "Theodore Roosevelt found the people bursting with pent-up righteousness, 'and what he thought he might require, he went and took.' "[4]

One of the most important measures of this period was the Hepburn Railroad Law, which extended the powers of the Interstate Commerce Commission. The railroads, deeply immersed in politics and all-pervasive in their influence, were at that time the most conspicuous target of the progressives. Anything that curbed the power of the railroad magnates was obviously a gain. The pressure group behind the Hepburn reform was the Interstate Commerce Convention, composed of powerful shippers of lumber, fruit and cattle, various Boards of Trade, and the National Association of Manufacturers. And it would seem that Mr. White failed to understand the dynamics of the Square Deal when he described these gentlemen as "altruistic" or "righteous."

Yet in that day progressives could appeal to every right-minded man. They were campaigning for justice, brotherhood, peace and similar vague objectives; and the battlefield was located, not in the economy, but in the recesses of the human soul. These were the noblest aspirations of the human race, and even industrialists who might be adversely affected by their realization could hardly disavow them. Nevertheless, it was impossible to make very much progress.

We found it necessary to bring our ideals down from the moral stratosphere. Who, we asked, would profit most in the realization of the progressive ideal? While everybody talked justice, some men obviously stood to gain by it and some to lose. We toned down the ideal, enumerating distinct rewards for the workers and the farmers. And these groups, indeed, have become the assured battalions in the progressive army. Oswald Garrison Villard relates in his memoirs that it was not until the collapse of the disembodied progressivism of Woodrow Wilson that he came to realize that the great hope for the future lay in the motive power of labor as a selfish interest group. Moreover it was about 1920 that Farmer-Labor parties, state and national, began to make their appearance.

This restatement of progressive ideals has had rather startling consequences. Justice is no longer a universal value. It is the private shibboleth of interest groups. Freud discovered that domestic ties had a realistic basis. Now the neo-progressives also found their realistic basis. For the configuration of labor and farmer groups has assumed the same relation to the fulfilment of our democratic ideals as the configuration of ego, super-ego, and id to the fulfilment of our amorous ideals.

The New Dealers were the first progressives to act consciously on this principle. They consistently encouraged the formation of trade unions, consumer groups, farm cooperatives and farmers' organizations so that they might have assured interest groups to support their program. Much of the trade union policy, Section 7a in the NIRA and the Wagner Labor Relations Act, can be explained in these terms. Here, indeed, was the impetus for the C.I.O. For when the A.F. of L. failed in its drive to organize the great industries on a craft basis, the administration gave encouragement to John L. Lewis and his C.I.O., which successfully organized them on an industrial basis. Mr. Lewis was not ungrateful in 1936. He lent $500,000 to the Roosevelt campaign fund in that year. But by 1940 Mr. Lewis, if not his unions, had swung away.

Like Dr. Frankenstein, while we have been creating these progressive battalions, we have been creating a monster that bids fair to overwhelm us. For they have a power and existence quite independent of the President, and should he hesitate in his benefactions, they might well forsake him for some new leader. Indeed, the whole structure resembles the Mexican Army with semi-autonomous units under the provincial generals. During the New Deal period farm organizations have become one of the most powerful lobbies in Washington and have consistently overreached their share in the administration budget. WPA workers have organized sit-down strikes in opposition to Congressional curtailments. And John L. Lewis has manoeuvered to undo his creator.

These developments indicate, I think, that the battalions were not sufficiently an integrated part of the New Deal. If Mr. Roosevelt had diverted some of the patronage which he used to coddle the old bosses of the Democratic Party and used it to keep within the fold the representatives of farm groups, trade unions, old age, youth, and Negro groups, he might have perhaps avoided some of the recent disaffections and succeeded in giving a more decided character to his party.

5. COMMUNICATIONS

Beside depending upon the political party with its dubious loyalties and upon the independent battalions, President Roosevelt has also depended to a great extent upon his direct popularity with the public. In spite of the weaknesses in the progressive army, he remains the personal messiah of unorganized millions.

Yet, even in this most primitive approach, he has been handicapped by weakness in communications. For it is all too evident that those organs from which the public draws its political information, are almost wholly in the hands of the corporations—not by conspiracy, but simply because the business of distributing such information is itself a large-scale and hence conservative business. Under these circumstances Mr. Roosevelt, the leader of the progressive army, has been harassed by difficulties in the chief lines of communication with his scattered and centrifugal forces. He has had to rely almost wholly upon his own personal appeal in the fireside addresses, which, of course, is considerable; upon the appeal of lieutenants Ickes, Hopkins, Jackson and others, which is less considerable; and finally, upon the appeal of his social achievements, "the propaganda of the deed," when the facts of these achievements could filter through the screen of newspaper hysteria and when the achievements happened to reflect themselves in gentle waves of prosperity.

It has been a difficult and irritating struggle. The constant thundering of opposition newspapers has had its effect in frustrating, not the hero-worship of Mr. Roosevelt, but his latter-day efforts at reform. After all, no army can hold together very well with its lines of communication constantly tapped and severed.

Something had to be done about it. There was no lack of indignation on the part of administration leaders. But that was not enough. When it came to concrete proposals, they were more reticent. Senator Minton stood out almost alone in advocating a reform of the "opinion industries," as Max Lerner calls them. He suggested that newspapers be held to strict accountability for the truthfulness of their reports and headlines. Cries of horror arose from the great organs. It required much courage on Minton's part, for a politician's career is very much dependent on the life-giving publicity that he receives through the newspaper columns. After all, if the press could be so exercised by the actions of the American Newspaper Guild with regard to shop conditions and the policies of the N.L.R.B. as to employers' influence over employees in union elections, there could be little doubt that the press would be excited by a threat of direct federal supervision.

6. DYNAMICS OF HEROISM

In spite of these weaknesses of organization and communication, the fact remains that the progressive army, such as it is, has depended largely on the cult of hero-worship for Franklin D. Roosevelt. This was implicit in the suspense over the third-term. A third-term was vital to the cohesion of progressive forces.   Indeed, the Roosevelt leadership is probably more vital to the cause of democracy in America than the Hitler leadership to the cause of Nazism or the Stalin leadership to the cause of Communism.   For those foreign causes are well-organized, and a shift in leadership could take place without serious defections in the organization.

We have had heroes in recent times, Bryan, T. R., and Wilson.   But we have only recently come to the point where the future of reform, in effect, rests on the triumph or defeat of one man.   The personality of F. D. R. has been our greatest asset in recruiting.   Like Napoleon, who, in victory or defeat, could muster army after army until he had virtually exhausted the manpower of France, F. D. R. has been able to muster voters in one election after another, regardless of the success or failure of his programs.

Max Lerner in *It Is Later Than You Think* recognizes the importance of this hero-worship in present-day strategy. He writes:

> "We shall be doing ourselves a disservice if we reject out of hand the concept of the leader because of the fascist taint that it now bears, or because of our fear of the power that leadership carries with it.   Every decisive group effort needs leadership."[5]

Take over the leadership principle for democracy, for the common man can only comprehend the progress of a movement by personalizing it through the leader.   And it is better that way, for

> "While the leaders and administrators are working out the complicated problems of economic control, involving changes of pace and shifts of direction, people must move in unison with them.   It is difficult, often impossible to explain the reasons to them; even if it were possible, it would be confusing.   Hence the leader-symbol: to bridge the gap between the needs of the state and the conditions of political education."[6]

From this attitude, of course, there follows the apologia for a third term, of which he approves if "a diminution of strength on the part of the leader might conceivably prove the decisive factor . . . in the event of a strong reactionary threat."[7]

But, it may be objected, the progressives are in a sorry state if they are so dependent on a single human being. What is to prevent Mr. Roosevelt from betraying them, from becoming an opportunist and selling them out? Actually, this hero-worship is not as dangerous as it looks. This is the most remarkable feature of modern heroism. The modern hero, Hitler, Stalin, Mussolini, or Roosevelt, by the nature of his idealism has little chance to betray his principles, apart from minor corruption. For the principles themselves have become so deflated, are so calculated to appeal to the lowest mass needs, food or glory, that he can find no other grounds on which to build his personal power. If he should fail to supply either food as a democrat or glory as a Fascist, he would lose his following and undermine his power. There was more danger of opportunism with the Mugwumps than there is with the New Dealers.

This, indeed, may sound paradoxical. But in order to be an opportunist, you have to hold some principle which is costly to your career, some spiritual integrity which you might sacrifice for material and personal gain. But with a deflated idealism, there are few spiritual values to start with and there is little to sacrifice. There is obviously less temptation for a rake to betray his ethics than for a Puritan. There is less temptation for a Pagan to betray his religion than for a Christian. And there is less temptation for an illustrator in the *Saturday Evening Post* to betray his art than for a Picasso or a Cezanne. Rakes, Pagans, and magazine illustrators do not ordinarily sell out; not because

they are better than their rivals, but simply because they
have so much less nobility to sell.

Many people have charged Mr. Roosevelt with opportunism.   They have pointed out how he has prostituted his
position for a mess of votes.   They point, for example, to
the "bribe" of the United Mine Workers in 1936, to the
pampering of relief workers and farm organization, and to
the various sops that have been thrown to the old age
groups, to the unemployed and to the Negroes.   What they
forget is that Mr. Roosevelt has not sold out by doing these
things; for the doing of these things actually constitutes
the major part of his idealism.   Moreover, in his resistance
to the veterans' pork bill of 1935 and 1936 he showed that
he was not distributing these funds in any helter-skelter
way, but was handing them out where they might do the
most good for recovery and reform.   Mr. Roosevelt can
sleep with a clear conscience, as can all who gear their morality to the wholesome animal needs of the community.

Now it might be argued that even on the deflated level
of New Deal idealism, there is a chance for opportunism
when, for example, the President shifts from satisfying
economic demands to arousing support for internationalism.
Foreign adventure with its strong unifying effect would
seem to be the last refuge of one who has made a botch of
things at home.   Here might be a way of shifting supporters
from those with stomachs to fill to those even more easily
aroused with a desire for national glory.   On these grounds,
both Republicans and Communists attacked the President
for having shifted his ground after the Munich crisis.   Yet
events have fully vindicated him, and many Republican
critics have turned about and attacked him for not having
gone far enough.

Still another objection has been raised.   What effect will
this political hero-worship have upon the national character?

After all, a President who is bent upon effecting economic reforms by any means at his disposal, including occasional tricks, bad faith and unscrupulousness, is no model for the young. And whatever may be said about the old Mugwump reform movement, it cannot be denied that it was calculated to improve the character of the citizen.

Dorothy Thompson, among others, has been particularly disturbed by this aspect of the New Deal. She pointed out that "though Hitler wants to make his people 'prosperous, free, and strong', there is not in a single one of his speeches the slightest indication that he wants to make them right-eous."[8] And she went on to argue much the same objection to our own hero. Hold up the monstrous F. D. R. as a model to the children of working people? What kind of people would they grow into? Institution smashers, Supreme Court packers, Big Stick wavers, and lusters after power!

For my part, I believe this is nonsense. What politicians have ever been an inspiring spectacle, except perhaps such occasional Mugwumps as Grover Cleveland or "Golden Rule" Jones or "Holy Joe" McKee. By their very nature, politicians are abnormal and unpleasant, busybodies who meddle with public affairs and are forced to fulfil all sorts of degrading functions. Each of the dictators of Europe, regarded in his own country as venerable and infallible, has undoubtedly suffered from the necessity of shooting his opponents, and, has accordingly lessened his moral stature. And if F. D. R. has been forced to do such a questionable thing as to attack the Supreme Court, it is little wonder.

It is one of the oldest and least remembered lessons of history that public life demands its own standards. As in military life, a leader may and very often must sacrifice his integrity as a gentleman in order to preserve the interests of the state, or of the nation or of the popular majority. He may change his plans without notice, giving out vague and temporary promises at campaign time, only to offer something more radical after election. Sudden surprise offensives are just as necessary in politics as in war. He may delegate unpleasant tasks to his lieutenants and then repudiate them, thus preserving the continuity of his leadership unimpaired. He may take rival and potentially dangerous leaders into his own camp. He may send up trial balloons, and when they have been riddled by the enemy, he may deny that he knew anything of their origin. He may even retreat and leave the vanguard, the trade unions, temporarily abandoned in order to preserve the main army of his electorate. And still he may remain a great and much beloved hero.

It is certainly expecting too much that our hero should be a model for the rising generation. Let us be reasonable. Inspiration comes from many sources—from clergymen, teachers, writers, musicians, poets, artists. Let them demonstrate the virtues and let them mold the character of our citizenry. Politicians have other things to do. Even so, F. D. R. is probably much better for the young than the conservatives of the twelve long years of Republicanism. For while he may be lacking in moral virtues, he surely makes up for it in *joie de vivre*, intellectual stimulus, and in contributions of relief milk.

PART IV

DEFLATION IN FOREIGN POLICY

CHAPTER EIGHT

On Seceding from the World

1. NATIONS AS ANIMALS

IN OUR attitude towards nations as well as men we are learning to recognize the animal underneath. A nation is not necessarily good because it appears to serve a good ideal, namely democracy, and another wicked, because it appears to serve a wicked ideal, namely Fascism or Communism. Russia and Germany are not alone in their naughtiness. All nations are animals, even that ever venerable organization, the British Empire. And if one conducts itself worse than another, it is largely a matter of digestion. For whereas England and France could waddle around with full bellies and a surfeit of righteousness, Germany was forced to bare its fangs in order to appease its hunger.

We have regarded nations too much as fully developed Christians. Whenever a new combination of powers is effected, we invariably catalogue their points in common and their differences as though it were a meeting of immortal souls. England and France could not be the friends of America, we have said, because they did not pay their war debts. Italy will not long remain an ally of Germany, we have said, because Italians do not like Germans. Or, in the same fashion, Russia can have nothing in common with Germany, for they are at extremes of ideology. But the truth of the matter, it seems to me, is that nations are not capable of friendship, and such alliances as are made are at best alliances of convenience.

If these introductory remarks sound hard, it is because they are written in the climate of the Fascist Era. The lesson that nations live or fall only as they have tended to their animal interests against the interests of rival nations has become almost self-evident. Yet when we employ this lesson as a standard for judging the ideals in American foreign policy over the last twenty-five years, we can see how much it has been ignored and how, in our attempts to bolster nineteenth century international morality, we have overlooked that jungle that lay beneath.

We have become familiar with the progressive's abhorrence of the demands of personal egotism in domestic policy, his concern for Mugwump purity and Puritanism, and his resistance to centralization of power. In much the same way, when the progressive has ventured into foreign policy he has attempted to angelicize the materials with which he is dealing. It matters little whether he is an isolationist or an internationalist. In either camp he has tended to leave out the unpleasant, but essential considerations, and thereby produced confusion or worse.

The progressive has been the most ardent exponent of democracy in domestic affairs. But historically he has been the least ardent defender of his country, which constitutes the context of the democratic experiment. Before the fall of France he took American sovereignty so much for granted that he rarely talked about it. He dismissed arms and empire as the concerns of the militarist and he debated American foreign policy over such remote points as whether or not the United States should join in crusades for international institutions, adventures in arbitration and collective security. Theodore Roosevelt is unique in progressive history. By contrast he was so enthusiastic for empire in the New World and for early participation in the First World War that his fellow progressives were continually puzzled and embarrassed by him. And in the perspective of the Fascist Era we are just beginning to appreciate his lonely eminence.

The extravagant character of debate in American foreign policy continued unchecked for many years because of our peculiar position among the nations. It remained inflated because during that time there was never any real threat to our security. With Europe as the battleground between a number of claimants for continental and world mastery, we stayed outside the arena. We had no compulsion to learn the arts of war and diplomacy. We took the precaution of a one-ocean navy only because of distant threats in the Far East.

Although we were happy in our security, we inevitably developed certain weaknesses. We lost the earthy touch in international affairs. If we were Englishmen, we would be reconciled to the diplomatic game, and we would expect our statesmen to take whatever measures were necessary to ensure our survival. And if they took us into war, we would not feel that we were pulling somebody else's chestnuts out of the fire, nor would we have to endow the war with the air of a medieval crusade. We would take up arms graciously and quietly, and we would fight for the King and Empire as we had always done, without asking too many questions. But being Americans, we could not act with such decision. Like Hamlet, we vacillated. Why? Because we were not sure where our interests lay. Every time Germany threatened a conquest of France and Britain, we were in doubt as to what was at stake in a German victory and what action we must take to forestall it. We had to make our foreign policy on a remote contingency.

With Germany triumphant, at least on the continent, the contingency has become reality. The arena of international politics has shifted from Europe and encompasses the world. We have found ourselves forced to play the diplomatic and military game, and our luxurious security has gone. With this shift discussion in foreign policy has taken a new and deflated turn. Our idealism is concentrated, not on achieving an unlikely isolation from the rest of the world nor on building a remote world order, but on defending the United States, the animal nation, on whose sheer strength depends the survival of democratic institutions in the New World.

In this book I have flayed both the isolationist and internationalist traditions, because I want to expose the phenomenon of inflation wherever it occurs in progressive history. Inflation of itself does not condemn a policy. I confess that I am sympathetic with the internationalists. I think that our participation in the First World War was justified if it kept Britain and France alive as buffer states between ourselves and a recurrently aggressive Germany. And yet the wisdom of that course has been much obscured by the League of Nations ideal which the internationalists added to their cause and which they failed fully to achieve. I believe that if the debate is conducted on the deflated level the relative merits of the two sides will become all the clearer. And the internationalist policy, if it is better able to preserve American interests and American democracy, will prevail.

2. HERMIT AMERICA

The foremost progressive exponents of isolation have been Westerners like William Jennings Bryan, Representative

Charles A. Lindbergh (the elder), and Senator La Follette (the elder) in the days of the First World War, Senators Nye, Wheeler and La Follette (the younger) in these Second World War days, and Senators Borah and Johnson of California, whose careers bridged both wars. To make the families complete I might have added Charles A. Lindbergh (the younger) but, of course, I am primarily concerned with men who have established reputations as progressives.

These men have renounced the animal nature of their nation. If wars have to be fought, they say, they ought to be fought out of complete disinterestedness and with completely disinterested allies, or else for last-ditch defence. Indeed, their moral standards have been so high that they would not engage in either of the two recent ideological wars. They disposed of Wilson's crusade because it was supported by the bankers of Wall Street and they have disposed of the present conflict in Europe because, as they say, England and France were not really fighting for democracy, but for the preservation of their own empires. All our recent wars have been "imperialist" wars. Hence, by their definitions, they have been relieved of any obligation to engage in them.

During the First World War they set themselves the task of removing our great nation from the wickedness and temptation of the world. They opposed all further increases in armaments. Preparedness, they said, would surely lead to participation. This attitude was not new. Progressives had traditionally been opposed to arms appropriations. But they had directed their energy specifically against any repetition of the Spanish-American War, against any further extension of our dominion over backward peoples. Now they continued this opposition on the edge of a conflict with our equals. William Jennings Bryan, for example, declared that preparedness was unnecessary. If the United States were invaded, he said, "a million men

would spring to arms between sunrise and sunset", although
he gave no indication as to who would supply the arms.
And he went further by proposing to remove the war-making
power from Congress and to restore it to the people through
popular referendum.

Moreover, the isolationists with their inflated idealism
failed to examine the basic factors determining foreign
policy. While they failed for the most part to foresee our
economic involvement through war-time trade, they had
no difficulty at all in seeing fanciful moral involvement
through the sale of munitions. It was all very well, they
felt, to keep the belligerents supplied with foodstuffs. But
by selling arms we were directly encouraging that Jekyll-
Hyde transformation of angelic nations into animal nations.
We were responsible for shedding the blood of victims of
international war. We were supplying the means by which
that war could continue.

Senator Hitchcock of Nebraska along with such other
isolationists as La Follette of Wisconsin, Works of California, and Stone of Missouri attempted to secure an arms
embargo in December, 1914. But the Wilson administration was in opposition and blocked them. In the spring
and summer of 1916, however, the movement gained
strength. Grain-growers and cotton planters gave support,
for they were unable to get shipping accommodations, because of the volume of armaments in transit. This time
Wilson himself, irritated by British transgression, particularly by the so-called "black-list", was very much tempted
to apply the embargo. But he held back, and in spite of
its vigor the movement failed again.

There were many other projects of the isolationists during
the First World War, some of them verging on the fantastic.
Henry Ford financed a private peace crusade on the chart-
ered and ill-fated ship, Oscar II. William Jennings Bryan

stepped down from his post as Secretary of State, deeply disturbed by the harsh tone of the *Lusitania* note, and joined the forces for peace. Such well-known reformers as Jane Addams, David Starr Jordan, Oswald Garrison Villard, Senators La Follette and Norris joined the cause. Most of them were sympathetic to the Allies and even favored Wilson's international objectives, but they felt, as Randolph Bourne said, that no ideal could be properly attained through resort to war and that the transition to a militant animal nation would do more harm than could possibly be compensated for.

Isolationist sentiment reached its height immediately after the Paris Peace Conference in 1919. Our experience with the realities of international activity had augmented the worst suspicions of the isolationists. England and France sat at the Peace Conference with the appetite of victorious wolves. And the kind of international order that they created with the League of Nations was of the newest and most deflated model, incorporating, to some extent, the assumption that nations were animals and must be held together by sanctions, economic and military. The assumption, to be sure, was well-taken. But the United States Senate, partly out of partisan opposition, partly out of personal spite towards Woodrow Wilson, partly out of concern for our basic national interest, but most articulately out of contempt for the animal nature of European struggles, refused to participate.

It was not enough that our entrance into the war had failed of its more idealistic purposes. We have been haunted ever since by a feeling of shame for having indulged in such an orgy. Indeed, fifteen years later, Senator Nye made an investigation and found once more that our participation had been tainted and fomented by the munitions makers. Senator Nye succeeded in getting a corner on the market of indignation against these evil men, and, as a result, we have almost forgotten that the essential criterion of any international activity is not the purity of motivation, but just the opposite, the degree by which it serves the national interest, and that the munitions makers serve as an interest group in promoting what is sometimes a necessary and progressive foreign policy.

3. VESTIGIAL INTERNATIONALISM

With the election of Warren G. Harding, the temporizer, over Cox and Roosevelt, the League of Nations men, it would seem that our concern for the outside world was nearing an end. But far from it. The Republican isolationists began to backtrack. Now that violence had subsided in Europe they overlooked the deflating experiences that we had gone through, and returned once more to the inflated internationalism that had prevailed at the Hague Conferences in 1899 and 1907. They dismissed the recent savagery in Europe as a moral lapse. They hoped once more to gather together a community of angelic nations, side by side with the less angelic League of Nations. In short, they tried to build an ante-diluvian world without any water-proofing, while a post-diluvian world order, based on actual flood conditions, was already in existence. Herbert Hoover expounded their position very admirably in a speech, November 12, 1929:

> "The European nations have, by the covenant of the League of Nations, agreed that if nations fail to settle their differences peaceably, then force should be applied by other nations to compel them to be reasonable. We have refused to travel this road. We are confident that at least in the Western Hemisphere public opinion will suffice to check violence. This is the road we propose to travel."[1]

Senator Borah was, perhaps, the most striking exponent of this vestigial internationalism. As I have already suggested, Borah was a veritable archive of inflated and archaic doctrines of American progressivism. Just as in his resistance to all tendencies towards centralization and the adoption of power strategy, here, too, he sounded angelic overtones to confuse the issue.

The first plank in Borah's program was disarmament. In 1921 he began agitating for a conference among the three great naval powers, Great Britain, Japan and the United States, for the purpose of limiting naval competition, the culmination of which was the Washington Arms Conference. This project, in the light of the time, was successful. It established the 5–5–3 ratio in capital ships, though it failed in a limitation of smaller craft and submarines. Even this modest *coup* was due to machinations of which Borah highly disapproved, among others to the negotiation of the Four Power Pact, in which the United States proclaimed its interest in the *status quo* in the Pacific.

In our later attempts at world disarmament we were less successful. Although we had been fairly realistic at the Washington Arms Conference and had scaled down our naval program only after securing some assurances in the Far East, we made light of the fact that in Europe France was unwilling to scale down her military defence unless she could secure sufficient collective guarantees of her frontiers. We offered many schemes at the World Disarmament Conference in 1932; but because of American angelicism on the one side and the rising menace of Nazi animalism on the other, the Conference floundered dismally.

The possibility of our membership in the League of Nations died with the elections of 1920, but the same issue was revived again in practically the same form in the agitation for adherence to the World Court. Again Borah arose to denounce both the technical problem as to how we might participate in the Court which was itself a part of the League mechanism, and the deflated idealism on which the system

was based.   For in extreme cases, he said, the judgments of
the Court might be backed with force.   Meanwhile, in the
midst of his opposition to the prevailing internationalism, he
was busy throwing up make-shifts of his own.

The essence of Borah's program was that the rules of
international law should be so amended as to forbid recourse
to war.   He proposed to erect a world court that might
operate very much as the Supreme Court of the United
States operates in cases between the states.   It would have
compulsory jurisdiction, and it would depend for its enforcement on "the respect of all enlightened nations for judgments
resting upon open and fair investigations" and "the com-
pelling power of public opinion."[2]

The enterprise, however, made little headway against
the more pressing claims of the World Court proposal until
1927, when Aristide Briand, at the behest of some prominent
Americans, proposed an agreement to dispense with the instrument of war in the relations between France and the
United States.   This, indeed, was the Senator's opportunity.
At once he went to work on a reluctant administration, on
President Coolidge and Secretary of State Kellogg, urging
them to draw up a formal treaty, not merely between
France and the United States, but multilaterally between all
nations, outlawing war.   By August, 1928 the Kellogg-
Briand Pact was signed at Paris; the nations of the world
agreed to outlaw war.   In a speech in the Senate, Borah
explained it as

> "a solemn pledge upon the part of the nations representing now
> practically all the inhabitants of the earth that they will not
> seek other methods than peaceful methods for the settlement of
> their controversies.   It may be said that it is not much.   I
> think it is a stupendous fact."[3]

If Senator Borah had based his foreign policy upon more
realistic assumptions, he would not have been so enthusi-

astic. Within a few short years one signatory after another began to bare its fangs; first, Soviet Russia, then Japan, then Italy and Germany. It was hardly to be expected that animal nations would abide by agreements that they had only signed in order to humor an American mood.

With the revival of the war spirit, with the appearance once more of the ugly fact of nations as animals, our Western isolationists became disillusioned again and refused to traffic with the world. They brought forward all the isolationist devices for which they had pleaded during the First World War. With the Italian-Ethiopian War in 1935 they secured the Neutrality Act, embodying the principle of an arms embargo. They revived the agitation for a popular referendum on war. They stripped us of our traditional neutral rights, and would have made us more hermit-like than ever.

Meanwhile, President Roosevelt was doing all he could in the opposite direction. Slowly, but surely, he molded opinion to favor the democracies against the autocracies— first, by the Chicago speech in 1937, pleading for a quarantine of aggressors; next, through frequent diplomatic exchanges with the powers of Europe, expressing our desire for peace and our support of the democracies, if they would only support themselves; and, after the war had broken out, by securing the repeal of the arms embargo in a special session of Congress. Through the gradual process of White House persuasion and diplomacy, aided enormously by the impact of events in Europe, he has secured support for turning the country into a non-belligerent ally of Great Britain.

At each stage in this transition the isolationists, Senators Wheeler, Clark and Nye have wailed that here at last was the definitive act of war. We did not go to war on any of those occasions. Indeed, those men have become outmoded; but they cannot even retire with grace. Their angelicism,

which was their highest recommendation in the previous
decade, has rendered them all the more fumbling and obstructive today.   This is the fate of men, not of too little
but of too much good will in the Fascist Era.   Their latter-
day efforts at isolation have been called acts of appeasement,
aiding the cause of the Nazis, and their historic works, such
as the Washington Arms Conference, have been branded in
retrospect as criminal negligence.

4. TOWARDS SELF-SUFFICIENCY

Yet, if the politics of isolation have left us all the weaker
in the present emergency, the economics of isolation, curiously enough, have left us all the stronger.   Many isolationists had argued that we would have less cause to become
involved in European conflicts if we became more self-
contained.   Now their hopes have been frustrated.   Even
by staying at home, we still play an important rôle in the
world struggle.   Such self-containment as we have achieved
on this continent is the one isolationist contribution that
survives.   And in so far as it serves the needs of the animal
nation, it is a great improvement over the inflated ideal of
free trade which the more fulsome internationalists have
made a part of their creed.

After the Civil War the Mugwumps expounded the policies of Cobden and Bright upon the American scene.   They
did not stop with the recital of benefits from the free inter-
change of goods among nations—low prices for consumers
and a generally higher standard of living for all.   The tariff,
they argued, brought positive evils.   It encouraged the
development of infant industries unsuited to American
conditions.   It raised the cost of living, particularly for
farmers who sold in foreign markets.   And without the
healthy competition of foreign goods monopolies grew up.
Moreover, with monopolies there came labor troubles.

The tariff was utterly indefensible, brought on as it was, through the corruption of legislators by special interests. E. L. Godkin had written in a magazine article in 1887:

> "Under the stimulation of the [Civil] war tariff, not only has there been an enormous amount of capital invested in industrial enterprises of various sorts; not only have mills and furnaces and mines and protected interests of all sorts greatly multiplied, but there has appeared in great force, and for the first time on American soil, the dependent, State-managed laborer of Europe, who declines to take care of himself in the old American fashion. When he is out of work, or does not like his work, he looks about and asks his fellow-citizens sullenly, if not menacingly, what they are going to do about it. He has brought with him, too, what is called 'the labor problem,' probably the most un-American of all the problems which American society has to work over today."[4]

Despite differences in economic and moral policy among the various brands of progressivism, there has been almost complete agreement on the tariff. The Democratic Party took over tariff revision as its special province. With every Democratic administration there has been an attempt to pull down the wall, to remove the whole protection structure and retain only a stump tariff for revenue. Grover Cleveland was a fierce and uncompromising tariff reformer, and went down to defeat in the election of 1888 on this very issue. Woodrow Wilson was another vehement reformer, who with the Underwood Tariff of 1913 successfully defied the lobby of the special interests for the first time since the Civil War.

But the Democrats were not alone. Progressives in the bosom of the Republican Party were often tempted to abandon their party traditions. Theodore Roosevelt, who was supposed to have stolen the fire of the Bryan Democrats, flirted with the idea of tariff revision at the beginning of his second administration, much to the horror of Senator

Aldrich and Speaker Joe Cannon, the Republican bosses through whom he operated. But he used the idea primarily for trading purposes, as a threat to render them more receptive to his other reforms.

In the fight over the Payne-Aldrich Tariff in 1909, the progressive Republicans of the West broke with the Big Business Republicans of the East. When President Taft, after promising substantial reductions in his campaign, encouraged substantial increases in Congress, Senator La Follette started a revolt. And though temporarily unsuccessful, the Insurgents joined the Democrats under the next administration and found revenge.

In fact tariff reform has been the program of all progressives of whatever party, not only among Democrats and Republicans, but among Greenbackers, Populists, Henry George Single-Taxers, and even among Socialists. It was not really until the inception of the New Deal that there was a split in the ranks. Such an inflated policy has often represented the most practical course in the light of the economic knowledge of the day. For it was still possible in the 1890's to combine practical policy with a very lofty conception of the destiny of mankind. The farmers of the West might seek to keep down the price of their industrial purchases through tariff reduction, while their apologists could chant the pleasant harmonies of the philosophy of free trade. Now such inflated political, economic and moral policies are, for the most part, no longer practical. Even the Western farmers have yielded ground. Long ago they decided that if they could not lower the tariff they would share in it. Such agricultural products as butter, meat and poultry are now protected by duties, and the farm organizations are among the most bitter opponents of the Reciprocal Trade program.

The doctrine of free trade, as expounded by Adam Smith,

was based on the assumption of geographical differentials, namely, that different types of production were best adapted to different countries because of the diversity of skills and resources. It was further assumed that there would be the most happy distribution of goods if each country produced only what it was best able to produce and exchanged these goods with its neighbors for what they best produced. There was to be a division of labor on a world-wide scale.

Much has happened during the course of the nineteenth and twentieth centuries to undermine these assumptions. With the development of technology and the further exploration of resources we found that there were a number of areas which were almost complete and self-sufficing without further trade with the outside world. The United States is perhaps the most fortunate of these areas. We depend on our import trade for only a minimum of goods—tin, rubber, wool, coffee, pulp, silk, and sugar; and we are increasingly developing these, or synthetic substitutes, by which we might become more completely independent. Other more or less self-contained areas have taken shape: the British Empire, Soviet Russia, the new Japanese Empire. Autarchy is, indeed, an objective of the growing Fascist Empires of Europe.

Whatever the progress in technology toward reducing interdependence, this progress, of course, has been hastened by factors other than profitable production. First of all, there is the concern for national survival. At the outbreak of the First World War it was sharply impressed on all the nations that none could well survive unless it had access to the raw materials and products necessary to feed its population and equip its armies. In the United States we learned that lesson well. Our imports of dyes and chemical goods from Germany were suddenly cut off by the Allied blockade. These goods were essential in the manufacture of drugs and explosives. In desperation we proceeded to organize our own chemical industry. And Woodrow Wilson, the free-trader, abandoned his convictions, at least to the point where he endorsed protection for strategic industries.

Second, we began to discover the disadvantages of building our prosperity on foreign trade. After the war, despite the fact that we had become a creditor nation, we continued to make foreign investments and to sell in foreign markets. Yet we made no provision for interest payments or for recovering those investments through opening up our own markets. Then came the collapse in 1929 and we found that such a policy had contributed to a flimsy prosperity and that it had produced no durable assets for the nation.

Third, in the attempt at recovery under the New Deal we learned some of the positive virtues of self-sufficiency. By public works appropriations and a certain redistribution of income we could create new internal markets to take the place of our vanished foreign markets. Moreover, the creation of these new markets went hand-in-hand with the processes of reform and it tended to make the economy more compact and more subject to government supervision. Now, at last, self-sufficiency was something more than a necessity for national self-defense, as in the first case, and something more than an escape from the unhappy consequences of foreign investment, as in the second case. It might now be a condition for a rise in our standard of living.

These factors operated in each of the great nations in varying degrees and in varying ways; and the development of autarchy in one country hastened the development of autarchy in all other countries like planets drifting loose from the solar system at the breakdown of gravitational law.

President Wilson began his administration with a strenuous drive for tariff reform and a return to economic internationalism. In contrast, Franklin Roosevelt began his administration by going in the opposite direction. In 1933 the World Economic Conference was sitting in London, discussing plans for the resuscitation of international trade and for stabilizing the major currencies of the world in relation to each other. At that time President Roosevelt was tempted to manipulate the dollar in order to stimulate business at home. Obviously he could not adopt both courses. He would have to choose one or the other. In a dramatic gesture he chose the latter, broke up the conference, abandoned the world to its own devices and exclaimed:

> "The sound internal economic system of a nation is a greater factor in its well-being than the price of its currency in changing terms of the currencies of other nations."[b]

5. CORDELL HULL: AN APPARITION

Progressives have become incurable pragmatists. We do not need and we do not use doctrines. In the field of domestic policy we drift vaguely from *laissez-faire* individualism to a kind of collectivism, applying collectivist devices wherever conditions require them. In the same way we must not insist on being doctrinaire in our foreign trade policy. It is not necessary that we be complete free-traders or complete autarchists. What is necessary is that we have some idea of our long-run direction. We should make up our minds as to which of the two poles is the more likely destination. Just as we have begun to recognize that collectivism, for all its deflated idealism, is the order of the day, so we should recognize that self-sufficiency, for all its deflated idealism, is also the order of the day.

Henry Wallace, Secretary of Agriculture, in a little pamphlet, *America Must Choose* (1934), explained the dilemma of the New Deal as to surpluses. If we disposed of our agricultural surpluses in foreign markets, he said, we would have to lower our tariff so as to bring in another billion dollars' worth of imports.   If we abandoned foreign markets entirely for a policy of self-sufficiency, we would have to withdraw some 50,000,000 acres of good farm land and transplant the uprooted farmers to perform some other function in the economy.   In either case, as he pointed out, there would be difficult and painful readjustments.

As a solution Wallace chose the middle ground.   He would compromise.   He would restore our foreign markets in part through admitting some half-billion dollars' worth of imports.   And he would abandon hope of ever recovering all of these markets through the permanent withdrawal of 25,000,000 acres from production.   At the same time he would attempt to increase home consumption for surpluses through various policies looking towards increased purchasing power.   As he put it:

> "Now we are trying a new method, a New Deal which seems to me to rest on irresistible logic.   We are trying to build up consumption per capita at home, as a substitute for the continual search for new consumers abroad.   Our new method involves a planned redistribution of the national income, in contrast with the unplanned redistribution that takes place regularly and usually unhappily, in every major economic crisis the civilized world over. . . ."[6]

This is a practical program, not free trade, not self-sufficiency.   In his desire to restore our foreign markets he was seeking the well-trodden path.   On the other hand, in his recognition of gradually diminishing markets and the necessity for absorbing surpluses at home, he was turning in the opposite direction.

Meanwhile Cordell Hull has made a great reputation with his Trade Agreements by which he has revived a little intercourse in a hard-shelled world.   To its practical effects there can be little objection.   Of course, the administration must utilize the remaining foreign markets for agricultural surpluses. Of course, the administration should encourage imports when American industry demands more raw materials to fill its increasing orders at home. Of course, the administration in pursuance of its foreign policy should make concessions to Britain, Canada, China, and the Latin American countries. But to effect a general revival of trade, Mr. Hull would pound rather helplessly at the barriers, the quotas and exchange controls, of the totalitarian countries that prevail in large areas of the world.

The tangible effects of the Reciprocal Trade Agreements since 1934 are hard to measure. Even by the official figures, it is doubtful that they have contributed more than $100,000,000 worth of business a year. Their most vigorous supporters do not base their arguments on economic effects. The Hull Trade Agreements are most valuable, they say, as a symbol. Here we come to the crux of the matter. Progressives cling to the free trade ideal as a symbol. A symbol of what? Not of economic and political realities, but of inflated morality. International trade offers one of the easiest methods of world uplift at the lowest cost. You promote peace, good will and international understanding through the simple and sometimes profitable interchange of goods among the peoples of the world.

Under the New Deal we have deflated many American ideals. Indeed, in the early days of the New Deal Secretary Hull was regarded as a back-number, an apparition of a tariff reformer of the Progressive Era, and much more rugged men, like his own subordinate, Raymond Moley, took the spotlight. More recently, however, with the declining vitality of domestic reform and the increasing concern with foreign policy, Cordell Hull and his Trade Agreements have come into their own. The ideal of free trade has flourished in the bosom of one whole wing of the Roosevelt administration, namely, in the Department of State, while at the same time, it has been deflated and contradicted by the actions of other branches of the administration, namely, in the Department of Agriculture and in the Federal Works Agency.

It persists as evidence of the evolutionary snobbery of the American progressive. These men refuse to accept the unpleasant assumption of self-sufficiency, that the selfish and animal nation must be the unit through which reform takes place. Under the ancient doctrine of free trade we assumed the ultimate brotherhood of man. Though we were blocked off from each other by splotches of color on the map, or by language or by national tradition, we felt that by the free exchange of goods we might join hands across these artificial frontiers. This was the means by which brotherhood might be fostered, and by which ultimately we could raise standards of living, at home and throughout the world. Progressivism, in its inflated form, was based on faith in the improvement of mankind. This ideal meant not only higher standards of living as an economic effect, but also permanent peace as a political effect. Indeed, it was one of the traditional free-trade arguments that as the people of the world became more dependent upon each other for essential materials, they could no longer afford the barbarities of war.

Now we are coming to the conclusion that the lot of American mankind can only be improved by a wall of tariffs a mile high for this country, or by coördinated trade policies in the Western Hemisphere. By adopting this ideal of self-sufficiency we admit the tribal nature of mankind and that man is not and will probably never be a world citizen. Under free trade all men were subject to our reforming schemes. Now only a certain kind of man, the citizen of the New World, and particularly of the United States is to be reformed and to have his lot somewhat alleviated.

We have modified the full rigor of this emergent autarchy by economic aid to Britain and China. But apart from aid to our diplomatic friends, the new idealism would relegate the rest of the world to its own economic and spiritual salvation. Let foreign progressives tend to foreign mankind. So far as we are concerned they are on another planet. They are beyond the range of our idealism. Indeed, by this secession from the rest of the world, we may do them considerable harm. By building our own chemical industry we may have hurt the prosperity of Germany, our former source of supply. By inventing our own substitutes for silk we may do injury to Japan, our present source of supply. By fostering the production of rubber in South America, as contemplated by Vice President Wallace, we may do injury to the prosperity of the East Indies. Moreover, from a variety of circumstances, from our export surpluses, from the flight of European capital to the United States, and as a by-product of our current aid to England, we have accumulated some two-thirds of the world gold stocks, all of which would make it increasingly difficult to restore the international gold standard which was once the corner stone of international trade.

It is an unpleasant prospect, to be sure, but, as I see it, one based on the realities. International trade has not done much for the cause of world betterment nor has it prevented imperialist wars. Besides, it is becoming increasingly difficult to maintain. Let us face the facts. For lack of a better device, we must employ the animal nation as the context of our operations, and such trade as survives must be carried on, not between private parties in the different countries, but by governments themselves through inter-governmental trading operations.[7]

It is unfortunately true that the Nazis and Fascists have made the most conspicuous use of the animal nation in the present world. But the nation can also be directed in the interest of a high standard of living. And let us thank heaven for that. For the nation is our only working medium; and if we could not put it to good use, we should be utterly without hope.

Self-sufficiency is a distasteful ideal. The conservatives in America have been building tariff walls since the founding of the Republic, but they never had the courage to renounce completely the inflated idealism of free trade. At different times doctrines of self-sufficiency were offered them. But they preferred to keep their ideals high and to get what they wanted through disreputable tariff lobbies and makeshift appeals. When they could no longer get sympathy for their "infant industries", they began to show concern for the wage rates of American workers. In this way, they served their souls and their bodies and made the best of two worlds. Nor would the progressives have adopted the self-sufficiency ideal, even under the impacts of the Fascist Era, if it had not been virtually forced on them as a necessary condition for other policies, for diplomatic isolationism in the case of Charles Beard and of Jerome Frank and for national economic planning in the case of John Maynard Keynes and his American followers.

Yet self-sufficiency is still somewhat suspect among American progressives. Even those who have been most enthusiastic are a little hesitant in accepting such a program permanently. Thus Stuart Chase squirmed:

> "Do I favor autarchy as an ideal? I do not. I favor a World State. But I must accept autarchy as the next stage in economic history, and console myself by looking beyond it to a sounder internationalism."[8]

And it is probable that between the two policies implicit in the New Deal most progressives are still on Mr. Hull's side. Maxwell Stewart of *The Nation*, reviewing the book in which Charles Beard first formulated his doctrine of autarchy for America, exclaimed in horror:

> "If Dr. Beard were only vague and confused, the *Open Door at Home* would not be such a dangerous book. But in coming out unreservedly for a nationalistic solution to American economic problems, he is playing directly into the hands of an incipient fascist movement in this country."[9]

Meanwhile the Second World War has given a great impetus to the self-sufficiency movement. At first it had been anticipated that with the victory of the Allies there would come a revival of sanity and free exchange. Now the Nazi victory on the European continent has forced us temporarily to abandon such hopes. Moreover, the demands of defense suggest that we supervise the trade relations of the whole American continent, despite the difficulties of competitive exports. The tensions that shaped our growing autarchy have increased rather than diminished; and the area of democratic countries that might participate in a trade revival has dwindled. More than ever, the world has been broken into sub-worlds.

CHAPTER NINE

Behind the Crusades

1. INTERNATIONALIST STRATEGY

THE ideal of a "parliament of man" is far more tantalizing and elusive than the progressive ideal at home, because, by comparison, the materials are so difficult, the cost is so great in blood and tears, and the results are so uncertain.

We should not feel, however, that everything is lost when idealism is lost. We should be happy that, at least, we have won the wars that we engaged in. And if we failed to achieve the ideals, that is a secondary consideration. For, I believe, world organization is the instrument by which the victorious nations administer the power they have won. It may be true that the "parliament of man" will never materialize until we develop a world citizenry to support it. But, in the absence of such materials, we must do the best we can through the dominant and interested nations; and their success must be measured in the maintenance of peace and the perpetuation of their hegemony. It is the purpose of this chapter to relate how the progressives have, on the whole, expected too much from international organization and how they have been successively disillusioned.

No one can deny the volume of the American contribution to international idealism over the last forty years. We were among the most enthusiastic promoters of the Permanent Court of Arbitration, created at the Hague Conference in 1899. We were highly instrumental in spreading the League of Nations idea during the First World War, and when much of the war idealism collapsed at the Peace Settlement in 1919, Woodrow Wilson still championed the League in the midst of the debris. We contributed juristic thought to the creation of the Permanent Court of International Justice. We sponsored the Kellogg-Briand Pact outlawing war in 1928. And in the Second World War an abortive international order was once more conjured up out of the richness of our idealism, the "Union Now" idea of Clarence Streit. Yet, on the whole, we have been much better at concocting these schemes than in participating in them. Although we joined the Hague Court of Arbitration, we failed to join the other creations, the League of Nations and the Court of International Justice.

We were very much the dilettante who, in times of crisis, loved to dabble in the affairs of the world, to give advice, and sometimes even to stick a finger in the pie. But our interest in world affairs was never sufficiently deep-seated for us to continue this participation when the excitement was over and the crisis temporarily settled. We tantalized the populations of Europe with magnificent visions, but when these visions were about to be realized, we withdrew to our own hemisphere. Although these schemes might have served the national interest through the preservation of peace, our stake as compared with that of Britain and France was so very remote that the American public was unconvinced and unwilling to give the necessary support. In effect, the intellectual generosity of the internationalists exceeded the popular conception of our national welfare; and this, in itself, gave us an unstable rôle.

In periods before war, as in 1900–1914 and in 1919–1939, a handful of progressive thinkers worked out long-range programs of thoroughgoing internationalism, schemes of collective security involving moral or economic or military sanctions, while the nation at large with its attendant politicians cared not at all.   When war broke out in Europe in 1914–1917, the nation and its politicians became so helplessly and irresistibly absorbed that the progressive thinkers could not rationalize the forces fast enough to give real direction.

For this reason, the expression "internationalist strategy" is absurd.   The progressives in the First World War were like pilots in a little boat that was being irresistibly swept over the dam.   They may have convinced themselves that they were going under their own power; and to prove it, they may have set their rudder and sails dead ahead into the cataclysm.   But in truth, they could have gone no other way if they had wanted to; and the whole demonstration of controlling the wind and current was dramatic pretense.

The underlying logic of our entrance into the First World War was, I believe, our stake as an animal nation in the survival of British sea power; and the incidents that determined the tempo of our participation were: the exhaustion of Allied credit for the purchase of our goods, the dependence of our prosperity upon continued trade, the relaxing of credit restrictions, the official Allied propaganda and the agitations of professional patriots, like Theodore Roosevelt and General Wood, and of the munitions makers, the interference with our neutral rights through the submarine warfare of Germany, and finally, the declaration of unrestricted submarine operations by February 1, 1917.

This was the current, and this the wind.   And yet the irony of the progressive position was that they boasted of being tough-minded and realistic, working with available means towards a possible end. They had become infected with the pragmatic philosophy of William James and John Dewey. Morris Cohen had written in 1916:

> "There are many indications that [Dewey's] pragmatism may soon become the popular philosophy of our progressive democracy—very much as the refined and almost austere simplicity of Epicureanism became the professed philosophy of the gilded youth of imperial Rome."[1]

But when these rising pragmatists went in for war, it was soon evident that they were employing an instrument that they could neither start nor stop. For a while they remained enthusiastic, pointing out that the war would introduce Americans to the problems of world politics; and with new problems would come newer and deeper thought. They even took credit for the declaration of war. Said a *New Republic* editorial writer:

> "For the first time in history, a wholly independent nation has entered a great and costly war under the influence of ideas rather than immediate interests and without any expectation of gains, except those which can be shared with all liberal and inoffensive nations."[2]

But the pretense did not last. Randolph Bourne upbraided them for forgetting their ends in concern for the means, saying "it had never occurred [to them] that values could be subordinated to technique."[3] President Wilson was so swept by the current that, for a while, he feared to expound the principles of an enlightened peace. Quietly he commissioned certain liberals to deliver his message secondhand in the large cities; but they were mobbed time and again. Harold Stearns wrote a few years later:

> "[Liberalism] must continue further its pragmatic analysis of events rather than stopping short when the analysis becomes embarrassing; it must continue to judge by results rather than intentions."

And he went on to describe their confusions:

> "The mind of American liberals, harassed by the glaring
> inconsistencies of events and by the stridency of popular clamor,
> gladly took refuge in the task of formulating ideal terms of
> peace. If one took a numerical count, for instance, of the in-
> crease of the "oughts" and "shoulds" in the *New Republic* as
> compared with these hortatory verbs before the declaration of
> hostilities one would be astonished at an advance almost in
> geometric proportions."[4]

Yet it is this very confusion and inflation of our international idealists that should be discouraged. More and
more our ideals are being geared closer to the realities of the
animal nation, and perhaps in the future we may be spared
such extravagant performances as we engaged in in the
past.

2. OTHER PEOPLE'S DESPOTS

Our two recent projects in internationalism have taken
the form of ideological warfare—the democracies against
the autocracies. This, to be sure, is not the first time that
wars have been fought for ideological reasons. In the
sixteenth and seventeenth centuries the Catholic and Protes-
tant countries laid each other waste on the ostensible
grounds of freeing the world of religious despots. At the
beginning of the nineteenth century a new crusade, compounded of liberalism and Napoleon, tried and failed to rid
the world of royal despots. In the First World War,
England and France succeeded in doing what Napoleon had
failed to do. But the work was hardly done when Lenin
set up an economic despotism in Russia. And what is more,
now twenty years later, England is facing and France has
capitulated to a despot, Adolph Hitler, who surpasses them
all, surpasses Catherine de Medici as a religious despot,
Louis XIV as a royal despot and Lenin as an economic
despot.

But ideology is not enough. Since in any war we have to invoke nationalism to defeat nationalism, we should not attempt to fight a war or promote international schemes, unless national interests are actually involved. From the strategical point of view, no nation, however advanced, can afford to enlist in every just cause in the world. The United States, even if Oswald Garrison Villard were President, could hardly have gone to war against Italy upon the invasion of Ethiopia, nor against Germany for the persecution of the Jews. And an ideological war, like any other international venture in which these basic concerns are ignored, is necessarily quixotic.

In the First World War it was not so much a question of democracy being threatened, as of democracy being essential to the larger goal of creating a new international order. The assumption was that democratic powers are essentially peaceful, while autocratic powers are war-like. This notion is very old, and no doubt can be found in the very earliest apologists for popular government. Tom Paine in his *Common Sense* at the foundation of the American Republic wrote that,

> "The Republics of Europe are all (and we may say always) in peace. Holland and Switzerland are without wars, foreign or domestic: Monarchical governments, it is true, are never long at rest: the crown itself is a temptation to enterprising ruffians at home; and that degree of pride and insolence ever attendent on regal authority, swells into a rupture with foreign powers in instances where a representative government, by being formed on more natural principles, would negotiate the mistake."[5]

So the First World War was conceived to be essentially a conflict between the democratic powers, England, France and Italy against the autocratic powers, Germany and Austria, with Russia and Japan thrown in to confuse the issue. In their formulation of the League of Nations idea,

American progressives lay stress on the fact that only democratic nations were to be admitted. Woodrow Wilson in his war message to Congress on April 2, 1917 said:

> "A steadfast concert for peace can never be obtained except by a partnership of democratic nations. No autocratic government could be trusted to keep faith within it or observe its covenants."

Here was the logic of the Fourteen Points and the slogan "Make the World Safe for Democracy." The Wilsonian progressives were not simply fighting to rid the world of one very insolent and aggressive autocrat. They foresaw that after he was out of the way the world could be organized by its peace-loving democracies, and order would be ensured indefinitely. They made it quite clear that they were on the offensive with their new vision, and that the defeat of Germany would be merely a stepping-stone to better things. This was the progressive aspect of the League of Nations movement, which was abandoned when the French, British and Italian democracies appeared as ravenous at the Peace Conference as any existing autocracy.

The disillusionment of the generation that fought Woodrow Wilson's battles can be largely attributed, I believe, to the inflated ideals for which they fought. The young men of 1917 were called upon to make the supreme sacrifice. If they had lost the war they would have been more satisfied. The Germans would probably then have reorganized Europe and the colonial world much as the Nazis are threatening to do today. Even without the horrors of Nazi ideology a German victory would have given the cause of progressivism a considerable set-back and would have imperilled the American national position. But the generation of 1917 would have been generally convinced that, though they had lost, they had lost in a valiant cause.

In the struggle for high ideals defeat is always much more

real and more sure than victory; and while such ideals may be good for a defeated nation, they are extremely dangerous for a victorious one. When men are called upon to give up their lives, they ought to have a fairly tangible idea of what they are fighting for. Enlisting Americans in the First World War was like calling upon men to fight for the pot of gold at the end of the rainbow. When they won they found that the gold escaped them. They demobilized at the end of the war, disillusioned and disheartened.

Our second ideological war, which we have so far been waging at a distance and without military participation, has been pitched on a lower key than the first. This represents no greater restraint on our part, but rather the impact of more severe tensions. We are not going anywhere so far as we can see. We are not looking forward to further blessings after the removal of Herr Hitler. This time we are on the defensive, actually and ideologically. For the Nazis have evolved a doctrine which, unlike the Kaiser's, is to be spread among all peoples. It is a cancer in our civilization that has to be removed, not for our betterment, but simply to ensure our national existence. This time the plans for world reorganization or disorganization are most effectively on the Fascist side, and we do not have to make elaborate apologies for a world of satiated and peaceful democracies. Whatever its faults, such a world is infinitely better than the one proposed.

During the Fascist Era we in the United States have been fighting this ideological war with words, preachments, diplomacy and with material aid to the democracies which are actually engaged in combat. Our idealism has been expressed in various ways in response to the development of Fascist aggrandizement from the Japanese invasion of Manchuria to the German siege of Britain. At first this idealism called for coöperation of the United States with the

League of Nations. Later the principle of collective security was invoked as a special kind of diplomatic dam
which, if applied with universal democratic support including our own, would have kept the peace and flouted the
Fascists without risk of war. But after the successive
evasions of this principle in China, Ethiopia, and Spain,
collective security was finally abandoned at the Munich
conference in 1938.

From the American point of view this anti-Fascist ideal,
though more restrained than the League of Nations ideal
of Woodrow Wilson, bore certain similarities to its predecessor. As the European crisis deepened, many progressives became hesitant about the possibility of another military crusade. Franklin D. Roosevelt, who had contributed
so much towards realism in domestic policy, only added to
the confusion here. He seemed little concerned over the
dangers of inflated ideals in foreign policy. At the beginning
of the 76th Congress in January 1939, in demanding new
armament in preparation for the trouble that was brewing
abroad, he became righteous:

> "Storms from abroad directly challenge three institutions in-
> dispensable to Americans, now as always. The first is religion.
> It is the source of the other two—democracy and international
> good faith."[6]

These words, falling on the ears of a generation that had
seen "What Price Glory?" and had followed the Nye munitions investigation, naturally engendered suspicion. Ernest
Lindley has protested against these spiritual appeals of
the President and similar appeals from the Secretary of
State. Lindley wrote:

> "A sector of American opinion has responded favorably to the
> futile indignation, the moral terms, and the grandiose references
> to international law in which the President and Secretary
> Hull have indulged. But there is another large sector which

responds only to concepts of national interest.   This sector, I believe, includes most of the World War generation. . . .

"Much as we deplored it, what Hitler did in suppressing
minorities within Germany and in overriding smaller nations in
central and eastern Europe was no direct threat to our national
security. . . .

"On the grounds of morality there is no valid charge against
Hitler which cannot be leveled against every imperial power,
including ourselves.   But on the grounds of self-interest, we
have ample reason to oppose Hitlerized Germany and to keep
a watchful eye on Japan."[7]

In the intoxication of their new rôle it would seem that
the internationalist progressives lost touch with the hard
and trying realities of an ideological war.   On the eve of
the conflict the Germans suddenly announced that Soviet
Russia had agreed to a non-aggression pact.   It was like
a bucket of cold water.   It was as if during the religious
wars of the sixteenth century the Catholic powers had
suddenly allied themselves with the heathen Turks in
order to crush the Protestants.   There were all kinds of
reactions.   Some progressives were relieved that Soviet
Russia now showed her true colors and that the ideological
war could continue against all totalitarians united.   Others
were bitter over the "opportunism" of Stalin, and unhappy
over the loss of strength to the anti-Fascist cause; while
still others exonerated Stalin, on the grounds that British
opportunism forced him into an early cynicism.   But whatever the reaction, the move came as a complete surprise.
And it suddenly dawned on many observers that nations
were not simply pawns of world-wide social and spiritual
movements, but that they had a life of their own, which
sometimes ran counter to the demands of ideology.

Indeed, the sudden reduction of the ideological war to its
animal components completely unnerved many progressives.   During the preceding years world forces had for-

tuitously formed a very neat picture, and it had been easy to make policy and choose sides. The domestic conflict between democratic and Fascist groups was nicely duplicated in the international conflict between democratic (and Communistic) powers and the Fascist aggressors. But with the defection of the Soviet Union the picture became blurred.

Now there has come the deflationary impact of the German Westward thrust. The driving power of the Nazis and the collapse of France came as such a blow that it is no longer necessary to argue our enmity to Germany on ideological grounds. With panic in the air, the whole debate has suddenly descended to the question of our survival as an animal nation in an animal world. We have become vastly more concerned over national defense than over the abstract merits of one side as against the other.

It has been the object of this book to show how inflated ideals have obstructed the course of American progressivism. In domestic policy they have mainly served to divert our attention and to waste our energy. But in foreign policy they have wrought far worse damage. Despite the realism with which we have been meeting the present crisis there are still certain areas of demoralization that remain as the battle-scars of our last foreign adventure.

Under the new tensions we have somewhat dissipated the fog of Wilsonian idealism and discovered that wars are still worth fighting, not for remote ideals, but for the preservation of national sovereignty. And the men who have been most bitter at the swindle of the First World War, like Walter Millis, have come to regret their disillusionment. For that disillusionment has left us all the worse prepared to defend ourselves and to check the threatening Dark Age that moves ever closer towards us. Archibald MacLeish has placed the blame for this disillusionment upon the intellectuals who were the worst infected with it and who spread it abroad among the people. Lewis Mumford has spoken of the "corruption of liberalism". But it is not the fault of the intellectuals or liberals. Rather, I believe, it must be accredited to the leaders who once sent a country to war under the banner of a righteous crusade. But these intellectuals while lashing themselves for their past sins are busy creating new ideals, equally extravagant, for the temptation and undoing of contemporary statesmen.

3. THE COST OF AN IDEOLOGICAL WAR

With the animal nature of nations revealed as the basic component of ideological war, we can now calculate just what is involved and what the cost will be. Progressives at war shift their allegiance from the movement fighting injustice at home to the movement fighting injustice abroad. Inevitably they must adjust themselves to the spirit of national unity and join in common effort with their traditional enemies—capitalists, imperialists, and munitions makers. Moreover, once they have shifted to national unity, they find it extremely difficult to shift back again to progressive disunity. Why? First, because nationalism is a far better medium for human pugnacity than progressivism. Second, because in the nationalistic detour the whole ethical structure of progressivism is usually undermined by the resort to violence.

From the sporting angle how can you compare progressive politics to nationalism? The former is really a very poor game. For one thing, you are never quite sure which side you are on. If it brings class warfare, millions of people do not know which class they belong to; and even when they seem obviously underdogs, they are still tempted to join the topdogs in their voting just for prestige. But in inter-

national politics are any native Americans ever in doubt as
to whether they are really Americans or Germans? And
are they ever tempted to join a European nation—except as
spies, red and brown internationals and Anglophiles?

For another thing, progressives are never sure they have
penetrated enemy territory, except by the outcry in the
Tory press. And even there the powers of Wall Street
are so sensitive and the structure of business confidence so
fragile that it is difficult to know whether a scratch or a
mortal wound has been inflicted. But when imperial
nations vie with one another diplomatically, the gains can
be fairly assessed by the number and size of the allies. And
when they engage in military action every advance can be
marked with lines and colors on the map, and they can
tally up their score in figures of square miles.

Again, what satisfaction has the progressive in a final
victory? It is true that politicians offer their followers a
"more abundant life", with more food, work, better housing
and living conditions. Yet an economy is a most intangible
thing to manipulate, and when a reform program has been
completed on the statute books, who can say that it will
really bring recovery and widespread bounties, and if it does,
who can say that the politicians really planned it that way?
Yet everybody knows that a nation has triumphed when its
armies have entered an enemy capital!

These, then, are only the most obvious weaknesses of
progressivism compared with nationalism. It is almost
like a debating match trying to draw its audience from a
football game. Which draws the greatest crowds and
evokes the loudest cheers? For which are banners made
and flaunted? And which rewards its heroes with the most
glamorous women?

But much more serious is the drop in ethical values from
the one allegiance to the other. The battles of domestic
politics are fought through orderly procedures, with only

occasional election riots and strikes, while nations fight one another half the time with intrigue and the other half with violence. This change in methods involves a change of assumptions, which is never more clear than in an ideological war, when the modest progressive takes upon himself to engage his country in mortal combat against somebody else's despot, and soon finds that he has created a climate in which his values can no longer survive.

Nationalism is a distinct road from progressivism; and although progressives may be forced upon it at times, let them beware lest they find no way off. For the highway of nationalism does not have a tough upward grade. It is not destined for any peaks. There are no visions or mirages of human brotherhood, of just distribution of goods, of a nobler expression of the individual in society. It heads downward, and after the start, momentum increases of its own force.

Nationalism, the world being what it is, has been deemed essential at times. In the life of our democracy we have had violent relapses from inflated progressivism to deflated nationalism, which have always tended to bring progressives down from the clouds.

4. THE END OF TWO ERAS

In the Progressive Era all institutional reforms ultimately rested on the belief that individual men would become increasingly generous and enlightened. In the development of international civilization reliance was not placed merely in Courts of International Arbitration or world legislatures, but in the moral improvement of the human stock. At the time of the Spanish-American War, David Starr Jordan proclaimed this principle:

> "The day of the nations as nations is passing. National ambitions, national hopes, national aggrandizement—all these become public nuisances. Imperialism, like feudalism, belongs to

the past. The men of the world as men, not as nations, are drawing closer and closer together. The needs of commerce are stronger than the will of nations, and the final guarantee of peace and good-will among men will be not "the parliament of nations," but the self-control of men."[8]

This attitude, as I have indicated, was also shared on the domestic scene. Was reform needed? Then leaders could stir the consciences of the people to the existence of the evil in their midst, and the people would rally forth as at Armageddon. Nor was there any doubt that all the world, if properly appealed to, would be on the right side. By 1917, however, evil was no longer ensconced in a few corporations or state legislatures but in the legitimate government of a foreign power. Now the clarion call of righteousness which had won so many elections between 1896 and 1916 seemed to have no effect either on the German government or on the German people; and so progressives had to stop trumpeting and set out for war. The progressive had never tried war as a method of achieving his ends. There really was no place for war and savagery in his whole philosophy; and it is well to record that even Wilson had his doubts. Here is a part of his widely quoted conversation with Frank Cobb, editor of *The World*, April 1, 1917:

> "I have never been so uncertain about anything in my life as that decision. . . . We couldn't fight Germany and maintain the ideals that all thinking men share. I shall try it but it will be too much for us. Once lead this people into war and they'll forget there ever was such a thing as tolerance. To fight, you must be brutal . . . and the spirit of ruthless brutality will enter into the very fibre of our national life. . . . Conformity will be the only virtue. And every man who refuses to conform will have to pay the penalty."[9]

So it came to pass. When you win over an enemy by preaching, you shame him into assuming your moral level.

But when you win over an enemy by warfare, you must descend to his moral level and prove yourself his match in all the tests of animality. This was the new ethic; and yet Wilson refused fully to recognize it. He kept right on preaching, trying to shame the German government into surrender at the same time that his army was busy slaughtering German soldiers. At every outbreak of popular passion progressives would point to the Great Moral Leader and counsel restraint. As Randolph Bourne put it:

> "The liberals felt a naive faith in the sagacity of the President to make their strategy prevail. They looked at him singlehandedly to liberalize the liberal nations."[10]

Along with the debasement of the progressive ethic there was the diversion of progressive aims towards nationalism. This was a natural process. The people in the street, called upon to fight another people's despot, found the democratic ideal and the admonition of "peace without victory" too abstract, and decided themselves to attack all "Huns" indiscriminately at home and abroad. It was now a question of national honor, and they were sworn to avenge themselves, not merely upon the German government, but upon everything German—the people, the culture, and all that they stood for. How could progressive aims compete with a massacre? Bourne reported that many who had never been stirred by the horrors of "capitalist peace at home" now had a large fund of "emotional capital to invest in the oppressed nationalities and ravaged villages of Europe."

Indeed, the war speeded up conflicts at home to such an extent and brought on such an atmosphere of violence, that between the radicals of the I. W. W., the returning veterans, and the raids of Wilson's Attorney General, A. Mitchell Palmer, there was little of the progressive spirit left. Harold Stearns made this the thesis of his book, *Liberalism in America,* from which I quote:

> "The emergence of clashing economic interests, which the war has done so much to further, has made mere "Constitutionalism" and even what we call "political democracy" more and more irrelevant in the field of action. . . . Exactly as liberalism proved itself impotent in the field of foreign conflicts, so in the field of domestic economic conflicts it is fast becoming moribund. As a body of political and international doctrine, liberalism has practically collapsed, and in that sense Mr. [Max] Eastman is justified in his use of the phrase, "the twilight of liberalism."[11]

Perforce violence on the right was met with violence on the left.

As this diversion took hold of the public Wilson stood by and watched his program threatened. It swept away both interest in an enlightened settlement of Europe and the processes of reform at home. It was like a great deluge that seemed to catch up and drown all the enlightened and emancipated idealism of the nineteenth and early twentieth century. Some, like Harold Stearns, who agreed with Wilson's objectives, criticized the way in which he conducted the war. He should not have become intoxicated with power; he should not have allowed the jingoes to preach hatred of the enemy; he should have welcomed opposition as a check upon his infallibility; he should have convinced Germany of the sincerity of our war aims; and he should have avoided conscription.

> "But we did none of these things: we crushed German militarism only to find that we ourselves had adopted many of its worst features."[12]

Some vindicated Wilson and came to the startling conclusion that something was wrong with the people. Norman Hapgood wrote in 1920:

"Let us not, in our disappointment over the outcome at Paris, forget the fact that ethical considerations will not down and that for the prevalence of those considerations, the President deserved more credit than any other man. . . . I say that this political conservatism of our people is a dominant cause of the President's failure to obtain all that he might have obtained at Paris. It would do us far more good to dwell on this national inertness than to overdue criticism of Mr. Wilson."[13]

But this attitude, it seems to me, is the height of priggishness: to blame the American people for what, in essence, were the basic miscalculations of the progressive mind. It is like the engineer who had designed a marvelous bridge on paper; and when the bridge caved in, he blamed the constructors who were unable to follow his designs and the steel materials which did not come up to his impossible standards. It is the common malady of perfectionists in whatever walk of life; as parents, they blame their children; as teachers, they blame their students; or as political observers, they blame the statesmen for not attaining their arbitrary standards. It is another case of our weakness for angelicism. For it is easy to strike a pose and blame reality——much easier in ethics and in politics than in engineering.

A good political thinker, I believe, should assume full responsibility for his ideals, and temper them to the imperfections of available leaders and of the human stock. If he is going to fight an ideological war he ought to know that men will employ violence and be susceptible to the deflated attractions of the nation as animal; and he ought to include these things in his calculations. Any one who sets himself up to direct the destinies of men, either in politics or on the journalistic sidelines, must assume the full burden. And when the calculations go astray he should blame no one but himself.

How well would the New Deal bear up in the hazards

of war? It is impossible to say, but probably far better than the New Freedom. For, as I have pointed out, the New Deal is considerably more deflated. The jump to violence from the evangelical reform movement was far greater than would be such a jump from the New Deal. It would be an overstatement to say that the New Deal has made a practice of class war. Since 1935, at least, it has talked much of disemboweling the minority of economic royalists, and such warfare as has actually been waged, even though constitutional, has been much more real than that carried on in the Progressive Era. We have handled metaphorical guns so long and have engaged so long in rhetorical explosives that the real article should come as no surprise. Besides, we live in an atmosphere that is already foul with the violent activities of Hitler, Mussolini, Franco and Stalin. Certainly, then, we should not experience the pangs of disillusionment we suffered after the last war.

And the deflated New Deal has another advantage. It tends to make our progressivism tougher in competition with the rival ideal of nationalism. After all, Wilson's ideal was made of flimsy stuff; it was not sufficiently diabolical. Today we are not resting our case on man's concern for his moral virtue, but on the selfish interests of millions of organized workers and less organized farmers and consumers.

The tasks that are now testing the statesmanship of Franklin D. Roosevelt in his third term are very much the same tasks that tested Woodrow Wilson in his second term. President Roosevelt is faced with the problem of militarizing the nation and fighting sabotage without provoking hysteria. He is faced with the problem of rendering aid to Britain and China without leaving the nation militarily vulnerable. He is faced with the problem of contributing to an enlightened peace in the event of democratic victory or the problem of maintaining hemispheric aloofness in the event of Fascist victory.

There are many pressures in one direction or another which make statesmanship difficult. Yet President Roosevelt has shown far greater leadership in keeping to his course than his forerunner. For one thing, he has the advantage that he can see the problems in the clear polarized light of a deflated idealism. For another thing, he has shown himself far more astute in maintaining the means by which he can effectuate his program. Indeed those who now charge that Roosevelt has been playing politics with national defense, just as they once charged that he had been playing politics with relief, are in reality paying tribute to his superior qualities of leadership. For it is the essence of a hero that he hold his following and keep his usefulness unimpaired, even though he must occasionally employ an animalic device. In times like these weakness and vacillation are the greatest dangers.

Nonetheless we must be under no delusions as to the problem that is before us. The era of reform is at an end. Our preparedness may be conducted in a progressive manner. It may develop collectivist techniques which may be used to enrich American life, but it is not in itself progressive. Universal military service, a two-ocean navy, procurement planning, suppression of Fifth Columns—these are the bitter necessities of national survival. The Army and the Navy have become the great consumers. Once our major concern was that our economy feed the mouths of millions of plain people; now we are concerned that it feed the armed forces.

But why, you ask, do progressives insist on undertaking projects which in the past have been their undoing? Why are men of such high purpose so often fated to play a part which men of a tougher fibre might have filled more grace-

fully? There is an underlying logic. One of the sources
of military strength in a democracy is the enthusiasm of
the masses; and in the nature of things, a progressive administration can enlist this enthusiasm far better than a
conservative one. For all the post-war disillusionments
that progressive administrations have suffered from the
Revolution on down, at least those administrations have
won their wars; and under the circumstances, the nation
could grant them the luxury of philosophic despair at the
framing of the peace.

In the Presidential campaign just completed (November,
1940) this was the chief issue that emerged from the fog of
charge and countercharge: The candidates, President
Roosevelt and Wendell Willkie, were largely agreed in
their conception of our perilous position. Nor were they
in conflict over the work of national defense, which, of
course, must be undertaken by the government, with a
measure of planning or war collectivism. Mr. Willkie
directed his fire at the inability of the New Dealers to enlist industry. Industry, he said, would only produce under
the stimulus of profits. And it was evident that, in spite
of his conflicting promises, he was prepared to cut off some
of the benefits that have been given to labor and to scrap
such progressive measures as tax and restrict the profits
of corporations.

Progressives rested their case on a broader conception
of the problem, believing that a fighting machine must
have, not only a large volume of physical production, but
also the enthusiasm of the men who do the fighting. And
the voters agreed that it was more important that American
preparedness be conducted popularly than efficiently,
though both would be desirable.

One must frankly admit that Herr Hitler has a great
advantage in this matter. He has built his career, both as a

dictator and as a conqueror, on the simple platform of German world mastery. No one can deny that he has fulfilled his promise on schedule, and until the Battle of Britain, ahead of schedule. When young men go out to die for him they know that, whatever the justice of their cause, it is a drive for power on an intoxicating scale; and such campaigns have invariably enlisted men for centuries. But when democratic leaders send their armies out, what can they promise? Neither conquest nor booty, but simply freedom as a nation and the continued operation of democratic processes. Here then is one great task for Mr. Roosevelt's third term: to make these blessings so vivid and so real that they will enlist an American loyalty as intense as that of the enemy.

References

CHAPTER ONE

[1] Dorothy Thompson in *New York Herald Tribune*, October 13, 1937.
[2] Walter Weyl, *American World Policies* (New York, 1917), p. 1.
[3] Quoted by Herbert Matthews in *New York Times*, August 23, 1939.

CHAPTER TWO

[1] William Allen White, *The Old Order Changeth* (New York, 1910), p. 30.
[2] Cf. John Chamberlain, *Farewell to Reform* (New York, 1932), p. 307.
[3] Herbert Hoover in a speech at Hartford, Conn., October 17, 1938.

CHAPTER THREE

[1] Lincoln Steffens, *Autobiography* (New York, 1931), Vol. II, p. 604.
[2] Quoted in Claude Moore Fuess, *Carl Schurz, Reformer* (New York, 1932), p. 209.
[3] Article by Carl Schurz in *Presidents of the United States*, edited by James Grant Wilson (New York, 1894), Vol. III, p. 158.
[4] Quoted in Fuess, p. 194.
[5] Quoted in C. Vann Woodward, *Tom Watson, Agrarian Rebel* (New York, 1938), p. 278.
[6] C. C. Regier, *Era of the Muckrakers* (Chapel Hill, 1932).
[7] Quoted in Regier, Chapter 15, "The Balance Sheet".
[8] White, pp. 53, 50.
[9] Theodore Roosevelt, *The Strenuous Life* (New York, 1900), p. 55.
[10] *Ibid.*, p. 44.
[11] Baker in letter to Regier, quoted in Regier, p. 198.
[12] Norman Hapgood, *The Advancing Hour* (New York, 1920), p. 244.

CHAPTER FOUR

[1] Woodrow Wilson, *The New Freedom* (New York, 1913), p. 69.
[2] Ray Stannard Baker, *Woodrow Wilson, Life and Letters* (Garden City, N. Y., 1931), Vol. IV., p. 125.

[3] David Lawrence, *True Story of Woodrow Wilson* (New York, 1924), p. 80.

[4] John T. Flynn in *The New Republic*, March 25, 1940.

[5] *Public Papers and Addresses of Franklin D. Roosevelt* (New York, 1938), Vol. III, p. 4.

[6] Oswald Garrison Villard, *Fighting Years* (New York, 1939), p. 526.

[7] Quoted in Robert McElroy, *Grover Cleveland* (New York, 1923), Vol. II, p. 213.

[8] *Ibid.*, Vol. II, p. 382.

[9] Quoted in Vernon L. Parrington, *Main Currents in American Thought*, (New York, 1927), Vol. III, p. 166.

[10] Editorial in the *New York Herald Tribune*, August 6, 1940.

CHAPTER FIVE

[1] Harold Stearns, *Liberalism in America* (New York, 1919), p. 70.

[2] Carrie Chapman Catt and Nettie Rogers Shuler, *Woman Suffrage and Politics* (New York, 1923), p. 134.

[3] Steffens, Vol. II, p. 480.

[4] Stearns, p. 68.

[5] Rexford Tugwell, *The Battle for Democracy* (New York, 1935), p. 178.

[6] Maury Maverick, *A Maverick American* (New York, 1935), p. 259.

[7] H. L. Mencken, *Notes on Democracy* (New York, 1926).

CHAPTER SIX

[1] Herbert Croly, *The Promise of American Life* (New York, 1908), p. 130.

[2] Quoted in Claudius O. Johnson, *Borah of Idaho* (New York, 1936), p. 188.

CHAPTER SEVEN

[1] Editorial in *New York Herald Tribune*, August 9, 1939.

[2] William Allen White, *The Old Order Changeth*, p. 64.

[3] Raymond Moley, *After Seven Years* (New York, 1939), p. 290.

[4] White, pp. 142 ff.

[5] Max Lerner, *It Is Later Than You Think* (New York, 1938), p. 299.

[6] *Ibid.*, p. 232.

[7] *Ibid.*, p. 231.

[8] Dorothy Thompson in *New York Herald Tribune*, October 17, 1938.

CHAPTER EIGHT

[1] Quoted in John H. Latane, *A History of American Foreign Policy* (Garden City, N. Y., 1934), p. 815.

[2] Borah's proposed resolution in the Senate, February 14, 1923, quoted in Johnson, p. 394.

[3] Quoted in Latane, p. 753.

[4] E. L. Godkin, *Problems of Modern Democracy* (New York, 1897), p. 115.

[5] *Public Papers and Addresses of Franklin D. Roosevelt*, Vol. II, p. 264.

[6] Henry A. Wallace, *America Must Choose* (New York, 1934), p. 31.

[7] Cf. Clark Foreman, *The New Internationalism* (New York, 1934).

[8] Stuart Chase in *Scribner's Magazine*, September, 1933.

[9] Maxwell Stewart's review in *The Nation*, November, 1934.

CHAPTER NINE

[1] Morris R. Cohen, in *The New Republic*, September 2, 1916.

[2] Editorial in *The New Republic*, April 14, 1917.

[3] Randolph Bourne, *Untimely Papers* (New York, 1919).

[4] Stearns, p. 146.

[5] *Life and Works of Tom Paine* (New Rochelle, 1925), Vol. II, p. 143.

[6] Message to Congress, January 4, 1939.

[7] Ernest Lindley in Washington *Post*, May 27, 1940.

[8] David Starr Jordan, *Imperial Democracy* (New York, 1899), p. 36.

[9] Quoted in Baker, Vol. VI, p. 506.

[10] Bourne, p. 88.

[11] Stearns, p. 25.

[12] Stearns, p. 24.

[13] Hapgood, p. 244.

Index

EDGAR KEMLER was a research assistant for the Democratic National Committee in 1940, Littauer Fellow at Harvard University in 1940-41, and professor of government at Howard University. He was a frequent contributor to the *Nation* and the *New York Times*.

OTIS L. GRAHAM, JR., who has provided the Americana Library edition of Kemler's work with a new Introduction, is assistant professor of history at the University of California, Santa Barbara, and the author of *An Encore for Reform: The Old Progressives and the New Deal*.